I can't think of anyone more q  ng
topic than Andrew Wilson. H es
of spirit and sacrament with r s
a fellow continuationist, I foun al-
together persuasive. As one who is less inclined sacramentally/
liturgically, I was challenged and stirred to think more deeply about
the relationship between these two aspects of Christian and local
church life. Regardless of where you land on these twin topics, no
one can afford to ignore Andrew's pointed and thoroughly biblical
treatment of them.

SAM STORMS, Bridgeway Church, Oklahoma City, Oklahoma

This is the book I've been waiting for! *Spirit and Sacrament* disman-
tles dichotomies that pit the good gifts of God against each other
and invites us instead to feast on the whole enchilada Jesus has prepared for us—through worship that is (I love Andrew's new term
here) "eucharismatic": integrating both liturgy and levity, deep roots
and ecstatic experience, formative practice and fresh divine power.
For what holds both *Eucharist* and *charisma* together is, at their
center, God's *charis*: grace.

JOSHUA RYAN BUTLER, pastor of Redemption Church—Tempe, author of
The Skeletons in God's Closet and *The Pursuing God*

Drawing from the richness of the Pentecostal-charismatic and sacramental streams, Andrew Wilson offers a theologically rich and
pastorally wise way of holding the best of both worlds together. Best
of all, he helps us find both grace and joy at the core. This is the book
we've been waiting for. It is clear and compelling, thoughtful and
pastoral. I kept thinking as I read it, "Yes! That's who we are! That's
what we do!"

GLENN PACKIAM, associate senior pastor of New Life Church, author of
Blessed Broken Given and *Discover the Mystery of Faith*

SPIRIT AND SACRAMENT

SPIRIT
AND
SACRAMENT

AN INVITATION TO
EUCHARISTIC
WORSHIP

ANDREW WILSON

ZONDERVAN®

For Samuel James Wilson
You make me happy when skies are grey

CONTENTS

FOREWORD

I spent the early years of my Christian life passionately in love with Jesus. I bought a shirt that said, "I heart Jesus" and wore it as often as I could. The grace of God flooded my soul (by his grace and mercy) and everything changed. The Bible was "living and active" and the verses would jump off the page creating awe and wonderment in my soul. I was truly reborn, transferred out of the domain of darkness and into the Kingdom of his beloved Son.

I also spent these early years in a good bit of theological confusion. I was reborn at a faithful Southern Baptist church that was serious about the Bible, did communion and baptisms regularly, and read the Scriptures faithfully in each Sunday gathering. At that time I didn't know anyone my own age that was as zealous about Jesus except for a small group of other young men I met at school. Most of them were from an Assembly of God church in town, and two of them belonged to a Church of Christ Church a few blocks from our school.

I'm not sure if you can imagine what the theological collision of one Baptist, eight AOGs and two COCs who were all passionate about Jesus would look like, but it was a mess. Thankfully, that never divided us but instead made us curious about each other. My AOG friends operated in a joy and energy that neither my Church of Christ friends nor I had seen outside of maybe a youth camp or other student event. I was surprised to learn that they also read their Bibles as much as I did and were experiencing the same awe I was. We wrestled through the tribalism of our local communities of faith that would vilify "the Baptists" or "the charismatics" as lacking something essential to being a Christian. Our churches would often offer a gross characterization of the others. Meanwhile, we prayed together, laughed together, worshiped together and visited each other's churches. We began to long for a combination of our communities of faith. I wanted the joy and energy of my AOG friend's church but felt deeply connected to something transcendent in the normal liturgy of my home church.

For the next decade I felt like a theological orphan. I loved and trusted in the Scriptures, had been trained in its sufficiency, inerrancy, and infallibility. I loved the Apostles' and Nicene Creeds and longed to take communion weekly, but I also loved watching people come alive in the gifts God had given them, seeing spontaneity in the gathering, and having excited anticipation about what God might do as we gathered. Most often I felt like the child of divorced parents who would bad-mouth each other, as I deeply loved each of them.

It was around 2003 that I stumbled across my first "Reformed Charismatic." It was as if I had found a small strand of gold in a dark mine. I have been following that line of gold for the past fifteen years. It is messy and marvelous, fearful and fantastic, difficult but worth it. Andrew Wilson lays before us a compelling vision of what he calls "Eucharismatic," which is a term that I hope grows in usage. As he skillfully writes, "The triune God is experienced in the church through the physical symbols of bread, wine, and water, through the Word read and proclaimed, and the presence of the Holy Spirit among us." Andrew is right! You don't have to choose. God has graciously given us the historic formalities meant to shape us *and* the wildness of the Spirit! I pray you enjoy growing in what it means to be a Eucharismatic and that more men and women might be formed through *Spirit and Sacrament*!

Christ is All,
MATT CHANDLER

CHAPTER 1

SPIRIT AND SACRAMENT

Pursuing the Best of Both Worlds

This book, like its title, is an attempt to join together two things that are frequently kept separate. It is a theological vision for the church that treasures all of God's gifts, the eucharistic and the charismatic, beginning with *charis* (grace) and culminating in *chara* (joy). It is a call to pursue the best of both worlds, an appeal to bring out of the church's storehouse both old and new treasures, so that God's people can enjoy his grace in Spirit and sacrament, with liturgy and levity, raised hands and lowered faces, confession and dance. It is an invitation—to Christians, to pastors, to *you*—to be Eucharismatic.

To many of you, especially in the Western world, I suspect this vision will sound like the worst of both worlds. I sympathize.

I think of one person I know who was inoculated against Christianity at age twelve, when he heard a man with an oily beard and big priestly hat, surrounded by icons, declaiming in tones of the utmost solemnity, "My heart is full, and my cup overfloweth"—and simply didn't believe him. I consider the absurd antics of some of the paper-waving, foundation-faced prosperity preachers who appear on Christian television. I acknowledge that much new church liturgy fails to acknowledge the realities of sin and suffering, and that much old church liturgy fails to acknowledge much else. I remember the excruciating boredom, as a child, of sitting through the same words being repeated in the same way to the same individuals every week, on wooden pews for wooden people; and the equally excruciating embarrassment, as a young teenager, of singing happy-clappy choruses to gradually accelerating Jewish melodies, as middle-aged women twirled their dresses, stamped their feet, and waved their tambourines. If eucharistic churches are dead and charismatic churches are ridiculous, then to be Eucharismatic would be dead *and* ridiculous, which is the only thing that could be worse.

On the other hand, I remind myself that children and young teenagers can get bored or embarrassed by almost anything— Shakespeare, sex, Mozart, fine wine, *The Godfather*—and that even the most captivating truths can be presented in either mawkish or soul-destroying ways. I reassure myself that there is not a church in the world whose services do not make some of those in attendance cringe, grumble, or both on a weekly basis. I reflect on the fact that bad ways of doing things do not mean they should not be done at all, merely that they should not be done badly. I cast my mind back through church history and recall the myriad of ways in which we have turned blessings into curses by making such a mess of them. I study the New Testament church. Faith returns.

Then I think about the possibilities for change. There are the obvious straw men. Contemporary churches that have thrown the liturgical baby out with the formalist bathwater and continue to proudly define themselves that way, even though their meetings are equally predictable and the formalist bathwater has long since evaporated. Or their traditionalist counterparts, where nobody is ever surprised, nobody (except the pastor) uses spiritual gifts, and nobody smiles. Far more common, however, are those churches that, through a combination of history, habit, and the avoidance of extremes, risk being stuck in Bible-church no-man's-land. Suspicious of anything

ancient (because it seems like dead routine) and suspicious of anything fresh (because it seems like a cultural fad), they have opted for
worship that is somewhere between twenty and fifty years old, safe
but anemic, predictable but ethereal. They are blissfully free of either
ritual or emotion, and as a result, they lack body and lack soul.

Some of that may be familiar to you. Some of it may even seem
inevitable. If so, then I invite you to imagine such a church encountering the delights of embodied worship for the first time. Imagine
them rediscovering the power of symbols: water, bread, wine, and oil.
Picture them reinventing their liturgy to include biblical elements
they have missed, and finding depths to the gospel that they had
almost forgotten. Imagine the snowball gaining momentum as they
use monks to help them pray and martyrs to help them sing. They
start to read books by dead people and find that they are more alive
than many of the books by living people. They catechize their families. They rejoice in the sacraments.[1] They do things that do things.

Then imagine them drenched in the Holy Spirit, prone to spontaneous outbursts of praise and the kind of joy that makes people
spin. They begin to heal the sick. They read Psalm 150—and actually
do it. They cast out demons when needed. They use spiritual gifts
in meetings—not just the leaders, but everyone. They shout sometimes and dance sometimes. They laugh like children. They pray as
if the Lion of Judah is on the edge of his seat, hackles raised, ready
to pounce. They expect God to speak to them at home or in the
office. Their meetings look more like African weddings than English
funerals.

Now put all of this together. Imagine a service that includes
healing testimonies and prayers of confession, psalms, hymns and
spiritual songs, baptism in water and baptism in the Spirit, creeds
that move the soul and rhythms that move the body. Imagine young
men seeing visions, old men dreaming dreams, sons and daughters

---

1 In this book I will usually use the word *sacraments* to refer to baptism and the Lord's Supper,
while acknowledging (a) that many Christians prefer a different word, like *mysteries* or *ordinances*, and (b) that many Christians recognize more, or occasionally fewer, than these two.

prophesying, and all of them coming to the same Table and then going on their way rejoicing.

Can you see it? That's what it means to be Eucharismatic.

You may well think this sounds irritatingly faddish. I can see that. To some observers, the charismatic movement is a passing whim, the *reductio ad absurdum* of the revivalist-individualist mutation within mainstream Christianity that began, like many modern superstitions, in nineteenth-century America and does not have sufficient theological ballast even to survive the twenty-first century without turning into a lurid and materialistic parody of itself. At the same time, within Western evangelicalism as a whole, "retrieval" has also come into fashion, as a largely rootless movement looks for historical moorings in the context of a generation seeking transcendence, latches onto anything that sounds mystical or ancient but still fits within its broad parameters, and then assembles it into a consumer-friendly bricolage of selected spiritual practices, devotional aphorisms, set prayers, candlelit vigils, ecclesiastical traditions (although usually not, for some reason, ecclesiastical authority), and monastic disciplines (although usually not, for some reason, celibacy).[2] Not only that, but what could be more faddish in the age of Google than coining a neologism in the subtitle?

Nevertheless, the apology stops here. The charismatic and Pentecostal movements are not going anywhere—their scale, growth rates, and influence in the Majority World will see to that—and part

---

2 Compare this with the comment of David Bentley Hart, *Atheist Delusions* (New Haven: Yale, 2009), 23–24, on New Age quasi-spirituality: "Here one may cultivate a private atmosphere of 'spirituality' as undemanding and therapeutically comforting as one likes simply by purchasing a dream catcher, a few pretty crystals, some books on the goddess, a Tibetan prayer wheel, a volume of Joseph Campbell or Carl Jung or Robert Graves, a Nataraja figurine, a purse of tiles engraved with runes, a scattering of Pre-Raphaelite prints drenched in Celtic twilight, an Andean flute, and so forth, until this mounting congeries of string, worthless quartz, cheap joss sticks, baked clay, kitsch, borrowed iconography, and fraudulent scholarship reaches that mysterious point of saturation at which religion has become indistinguishable from interior decorating." It would not be difficult to frame a similar list for pop evangelicalism.

of the argument of what follows is precisely that the historic church has always been more "charismatic" than either cautious conservatives or sectarian enthusiasts have been willing to admit. Retrieval, admittedly, is in vogue, but it is worth asking why. My suspicion is that much of it stems from a genuine sense, most acute in charismatic and "low" evangelical churches, that we must have some theological heritage somewhere, and that if the church of Jesus Christ is one body, the other guys cannot always have been totally wrong about everything (the flip side of which, fitting nicely with the impulse of postmodernity, is that our guys cannot always have been totally right about everything).[3] Neologisms, as silly as they sometimes are when used for branding purposes, can be provocative in the best sense, simply by juxtaposing ideas that do not usually sit alongside each other. They also—one thinks of *banana republic, metrosexual, différance, meme,* and so on—have the power to encapsulate a paragraph in a few syllables, which I hope is also true in this case. So: Eucharismatic it is.

That said, like any new term, it probably needs a bit of explanation. By *eucharistic* I obviously mean to refer to the celebration of the Eucharist (or Communion, or the Lord's Supper) in corporate worship. But I also mean to evoke the entire Christian tradition in which it plays a central role. When I see a church notice board proclaiming that it has a "sung Eucharist at 10:00 every Sunday," I know rather more than that the congregation comes together at some stage to share bread and wine. Somehow, the word is richer than that. I assume that the service includes some combination of prayers, formal liturgy, confession, hymns, psalms, readings, silence, sermon, offering, benediction, and commission. I also assume that it does not include spontaneous spiritual gifts, lengthy times of extended corporate singing, sermons that last more than twenty minutes, video presentations, or ministry times. That, in turn, says something about the way the church conceives of itself, as heirs of the catholic

---

3 For an insightful recent analysis of the quest for antiquity in contemporary (especially American) evangelicalism, see Kenneth Stewart, *In Search of Ancient Roots* (Downers Grove: IVP, 2017).

tradition, with all its history and depth, as well as its shortcomings. (I am distinguishing here between *catholic*, which simply refers to the universal church across time, and *Roman Catholic*, which refers to the Church of Rome.) To be eucharistic, in this sense, is more than merely to celebrate the Eucharist, although it is certainly not less. It is to be historically rooted, unashamedly sacramental, deliberately liturgical, and self-consciously catholic.

The word *charismatic* has an even wider range of resonances. In its narrowest form, to be charismatic means to be part of a church that traces its roots to the charismatic movement of the 1960s and 1970s, often as distinct from the Pentecostal movement (usually dated from 1906). More casually, and inaccurately, the word is sometimes used to describe churches with a contemporary and expressive form of worship, so that a church could seem "charismatic" for having a band on the stage and extended times of singing, raised hands and dancing, even if most of the *charismata* never made an appearance. More often, *charismatic* is a bucket term for any contemporary church that emphasizes the reality of supernatural experiences and the availability of the New Testament gifts of the Holy Spirit to ordinary believers today: speaking in other languages, prophecy, healing, miracles, and so on. In its broadest sense, it can also connote a particular type of experiential, pietist, or mystical Christianity, in which personal and deeply emotional encounters with God occur, and a clear and direct sense of God's presence and communication is felt by the worshiper.[4] Given this diversity, it is probably worth specifying that I have the last two of these meanings in mind (use of the gifts and experientialism), rather than the first two (emerging from the 1970s, and contemporary in style). Whatever our denominational origins, to be charismatic is to expect spiritual experience, pursue and use the *charismata*, live and pray as if angels and demons are real, and express worship to God with all the joy and exuberance of a Hallel psalmist.

---

4   When a church historian describes a group of pietist, seventeenth-century Roman Catholics as "kind of charismatic," for example, we know exactly what he means (Professor Carl Trueman in his lectures on the Reformation at Westminster Theological Seminary, part 33, on Blaise Pascal and the Jansenists).

As such, I am using these words in their positive senses. Sadly, we do not have to go far to find both labels, and anyone who lays claim to them, being damned by association with legalists, loons, dinosaurs, profiteers, papists, jargon mongers, charlatans, bores, sentimentalists, heretics, idolaters, or oddballs. In response, we could say that similar things are true of the word *Christian*, or for that matter the word *human*; we could note that none of these stereotypes come within a country mile of what Paul meant by *eucharisteō* ("I thank") or *charismata* ("grace gifts"); and we could point out that to abstain from all English words with unfortunate connotations would be to commit to an unintentional vow of silence, even if (especially if!) we are talking theologically.

A more important reason to use the terms positively, however, is the fact that the people with the most jaundiced view of charismatics are the ones who are most in need of seeing what they bring to the party, and it is those least likely to use the word *Eucharist* that are also least likely to drink deeply from the wells of the church's history. Part of the point of bringing them together, with God's grace, his *charis*, at the center, is to highlight how much these two traditions, in their most biblical expressions, can and should have in common.

To be Eucharismatic, then, is to hold to the hope that it is possible to have one's ecclesiological cake and eat it. There is no reason, beyond a series of historical accidents, why there cannot be churches in which set prayers are followed by spontaneous prophecies, and the "altar call" summons people to the Communion Table, and the rhythmic recital of the Nicene Creed builds into an explosion of musical celebration, with dancing in the aisles and angels in the architecture. That is the vision that this book is trying to cast, and I am convinced—and hope to convince you—that the pursuit of it will make our worship richer, our churches deeper, and our joy greater. Since all theology, as Robert Jenson puts it, "must be written for the undivided church that the Spirit will someday grant," I think it is probably worth the attempt.[5]

---

5 Robert Jenson, "A Theological Autobiography, to Date," in *Dialog: A Journal of Theology* 46.1 (2007): 46–54.

🔥 🔥 🔥

One thing is worth clarifying before we go any further: in what follows, I take it as read that the Bible is true, inspired, authoritative, sufficient, and at the heart of the Christian life. This might sound too obvious to need mentioning, given my (presumably) broadly evangelical audience, but two things prompt me to mention it here.

The first is a matter of focus. This book is written to persuade people that it is possible, and desirable, to be spiritual and sacramental at the same time; it is not written to persuade people that we should be scriptural as well. Although others have written books that combine all three of these, that is not my aim here.[6] But this could imply that I think sacraments and spiritual gifts are somehow more important than Scriptures, which would be a disaster. On the contrary: it is only by seeing Scripture as Jesus did—as God's authoritative, inspired, unbreakable, coherent, clear, sufficient Word—that we have any grounds at all to insist that we should worship in a particular way or eagerly desire spiritual gifts.[7] If Scripture is not true, then the rest of this book can be met with a nonchalant shrug. The Eucharismatic house is built on evangelical foundations.

The second is that both the eucharistic and charismatic traditions contain elements that can, if we are not careful, lead to a certain squishiness on the doctrine of Scripture.[8] Sacramental and liturgical Christianity has a beautiful, deep, theologically rich history, but

---

6 Lesslie Newbigin, *The Household of God* (London: SCM Press, 1953), speaks of Protestant, Catholic, and Pentecostal; his ideas are picked up on by Gordon T. Smith, *Evangelical, Sacramental & Pentecostal: Why the Church Should Be All Three* (Downers Grove: IVP, 2017). A different proposal comes in David Pawson's *The Normal Christian Birth* (London: Hodder & Stoughton, 1997), who identifies liberal, evangelical, sacramental, and Pentecostal emphases in Christian initiation.

7 I make the case for this view of Scripture in my little book *Unbreakable: What the Son of God Said about the Word of God* (Leyland: 10Publishing, 2014).

8 Nobody saw this more clearly than Martin Luther, although he would certainly have stated the matter more strongly than this. He regarded both the papists (the Roman Catholic Church that was trying to silence him) and the spiritualists (fanatics like the Zwickau prophets, Thomas Müntzer, and his former colleague Andreas Karlstadt) as falling into the same error—that of believing that they could experience the work of the Spirit without the Word—and thought both would inevitably lead to a loss of the gospel of grace.

in some contexts this has become a source of authority alongside Scripture, rather than a valued and time-honored reading of it. In charismatic churches, the threat is different: it is not so much the Bible's unique authority as its unique sufficiency that can be (and has been) relegated in the pursuit of miraculous gifts and experiences. The result is that, with some justification, many in the church today regard either eucharistic or charismatic traditions (or both!) as potentially wobbly on the Bible. In that context, without a robust commitment to Scripture, the invitation to be Eucharismatic could quickly become a thoroughly self-defeating double whammy.

The Triune God is experienced in the church through the physical symbols of bread, wine, and water, through the Word read and proclaimed, and through the activity and presence of the Holy Spirit amongst us. The three are interconnected, like Christmas, Easter, and Pentecost, each illuminating and making sense of one another. If one is marginalized, the other two ultimately suffer. So it seems sensible, at the start of a book about two of them, to spell out the centrality of the third one. Like the disciples in Luke 24, we experience God as the Father clothes us with his Spirit, as Jesus is made known to us in the breaking of the bread—and as our hearts burn within us as he opens to us the Scriptures.[9]

So where exactly are we going?

Like Paul's letters, and Christian thought as a whole, we begin with *charis*, or grace (chapter 2). The grace of God stands at the heart of all Christian experience, and the theological foundation for all that follows is the idea that God is fundamentally a gift giver, and consequently that our joy in him flows most naturally when we make as much use of as many of his gifts as we can. To that end, we start by laying out a brief theology of divine gifts, and then considering how

---

9   Luke 24:32, 35, 49.

we best respond to them, before touching on some implications for our corporate worship.

The next chapter focuses on *chara*—joy—and how to achieve it (chapter 3). Despite the noisy delight that resounds from the pages of Scripture, the church has not always looked as happy and hopeful as the apostles said we would be, and that should prompt us to pause and ask why. Having said that, we cannot be satisfied by an anemic, Christianized, don't-worry-be-happy routine either; it must be possible to lament and celebrate, be serious and joyful, at the same time. It is important to consider how this kind of both/and can be cultivated and how being Eucharismatic can help us.

We then move on to think about how being eucharistic, in the broad sense we have defined it here, brings richness, depth, and happiness to our worship (chapter 4). For many believers and churches today, repetition feels inauthentic and a high view of symbols feels magical. But the catholic tradition, the liturgical history of the church, and of course the sacraments are gifts from God, and the best way of responding to gifts from God is to enjoy them, thankfully and gleefully. This chapter aims to persuade those for whom the words *sacrament* and *liturgy* sound dead and deathly that there is joy, depth, and life to be found there.

Then we will make a similar case for being charismatic (chapter 5). In much of the Western church, at least, various gifts that the New Testament church seem to have used freely have all-but-disappeared, because they are regarded as no longer available today (or, alternatively, because people are not quite sure how to pursue them and use them without becoming weird). So this chapter offers a strong defense of the continuation of the *charismata* and calls for us to pursue both the gifts and the experience of the Holy Spirit.

Finally, we will bring these two strands together and reflect on how Eucharismatic practice might look today (chapter 6). Local application will obviously be shaped by a range of factors including history, theology, tradition, contextualization, diversity, and gift, but it should at least be possible to sketch some ways in which we might pursue the best of both worlds while remaining mindful of the many challenges in doing so. This last chapter takes us back to the first Eucharismatic church we know about, the New Testament church, and gives ten suggestions for cultivating similar practice today.

We begin, however, where the gospel does, and in fact where creation does. We begin with grace.

CHAPTER 2

CHARIS

A Theology of Gift

In an important sense, all Christian theology is charismatic. Every doctrine we have concerns a grace-gift of some sort, with the exception of our doctrine of God, which, of course, concerns the Giver. Creation, life, sex, fall, promise, seed, covenant, Israel, redemption, Law, land, temple, kingdom, hope, incarnation, cross, resurrection, Spirit, gospel, church, sacraments, prayer, Scriptures, judgment, new creation—whatever theological topics we discuss, and however we arrange them, we will find gift at the heart of all of them. Christianity is gracious from beginning to end. I would be tempted to call it Charistianity, if I hadn't played my neologism card already.

One happy side effect of this is that, if we are not sure how to respond to, say, sacramental or spiritual gifts, we can draw on a rich seam of biblical teaching about gifts to help us. On every page of Scripture, we will find wisdom on how to identify God's gifts, how to think about them, and how to respond to them. They are gifts, not rewards. They are to be received, not earned. They are to be enjoyed, not worshiped. Most obviously, they are always very good.

Existence itself is a gift. The creation story is full of gifts. Life is given to creatures. Earth is given to humanity. Woman is given to man. Children are given to woman. Despite our preoccupation with the one tree that was not given to humanity, Genesis draws our attention to the multitudes that were: "Behold, I have given you every plant yielding seed that is on the face of all the earth, and every tree with seed in its fruit" (Genesis 1:29). Raspberries, olives, lemons, rosemary, garlic, mangoes, cocoa. Then a few chapters later, the animals are thrown in as well: "As I gave you the green plants, I give you everything" (9:3). Honey, duck eggs, cream, roast lamb, rainbow trout, filet mignon. "Everything."

God gives humans dominion over all of creation: mountain ranges and waterfalls, deserts and jungles, leopards, glaciers, sequoias, oranges, peacocks. He gives rain. He gives light. He gives fragrances and flavors, even though, as a spiritual being himself, he has neither a nose nor a tongue. He gives colors. (Most of us, I suspect, have never considered the theological implications of the existence of purple.) He covers the earth with food-giving plants or life-giving water, and in the places where he doesn't, the very rocks cry out. He creates orgasms and oxygen. None of these things are needed by God or deserved by his creatures, but he gives them anyway. Creation is *charis*.

The serpent, by contrast, has nothing to give. So he focuses his attack on undermining God's gifts, first by insinuating they haven't really been given at all ("Did he really say you can't eat *anything*?") and then by suggesting that God's motives are sinister ("He's just worried you'll become godlike, you see"). It is hard to believe that anyone on safari in the Serengeti would complain that there were no sand flies, or a diner at Le Gavroche would lament the lack of spam fritters on the menu, but their eyes move from the abundance all around them to the one thing God hasn't given. They desire it. They eat. They die. The fall is what happens when we think God's gifts aren't good enough.

The gifts keep on coming anyway. He gives the promise that one day the seed, the snake crusher, will come. He gives clothes. He gives Eve sons: Cain, Abel, and Seth. He gives the world an ark, a covenant, and a rainbow. He gives Abram a name, a seed, a blessing, and a land, and the name is great, the seed is everlasting, the blessing is for every nation, and the land flows with milk and honey. He gives children to barren women and inheritances to undeserving men. He gives reminders of his promises continually: through angelic visitors and wrestling matches, rams and lambs, in bushes and up ladders, in clouds and fire. He gives freedom from slavery, manna from heaven, water from rock, and forgiveness from sin. He gives prophets and priests, tabernacle and Torah, exodus and empire.

It is worth noting a surprising but often neglected fact at this point: these gifts are not ambiguous. In Hesiod and Homer, the first great poets of European civilization, gifts are two-sided, tricksy, even booby-trapped. The gift of fire backfires. The gift of woman— Pandora, whose name means "all gift"—is given as a *kalon kakon*, a "beautiful evil," bringing both life and affliction. Her famous wedding present from Zeus is a jar (or box) that he instructs her to keep shut, but when opened, it releases pain, death, misery, and pestilence. A giant horse is given to honor the Trojans, but it hides an army inside, and the city falls. *Timeo danaos et dona ferentes*, as Virgil wrote: "I fear the Greeks, and those who bear gifts."[1] In the Greek and Roman foundation myths, the ambiguity of gift is proverbial.

God's gifts, by contrast, are unequivocally good. Creation, according to Genesis 1, is good, good, good, good, very good. The garden is a paradise. Work is good, sex is good, marriage is good. Despite Adam's Promethean efforts to spin the fall as if it was somehow a problem with the gifts, or even the Giver—"The woman you gave me, she gave me the fruit, and I ate it"—it patently wasn't; there are no Greek-style

---

1 Virgil, *Aeneid* II.49. I owe the point in this paragraph to Peter Leithart, *Heroes of the City of Man: A Christian Guide to Select Ancient Literature* (Moscow: Canon Press, 1999), 57–59.

landmines in the garden of grace. The rainbow guarantees goodness forever. The covenant with Abraham concerns the blessing of
the entire world, and to read the rest of the Old Testament is to follow that blessing down the generations with all its surprising twists
and turns, like watching a cups-and-balls routine, only stranger, and
invariably good. The law is good, reviving the soul. The land is good,
with grape clusters the size of wheelie bins. The temple is good, the
joy of the whole earth. There are no Trojan horses, beautiful evils, or
jars of death here, no secret miseries hidden in the small print. When
God gives, it is for the blessing of everybody.

Never is this truer than it is of Jesus. What can be given that com-
pares with God himself? The incarnation is the most extravagant gift
in all history or literature, and the nativity stories draw out this point
in a variety of ways, from the subtle ("Greetings, O favored one, the
Lord is with you"[2]), to the suggestive ("Then, opening their treasures,
they offered him gifts"[3]), to the blatant ("From his fullness we have
all received, grace upon grace."[4]) The original Christmas present,
wrapped in muslins and rags rather than in decorative paper, does
not merely come to give; he is himself a gift, the gift, the most outlandish demonstration of love that God could possibly offer. Everything he
gives to the crowds who follow him—good news, sight, speech, ritual
cleanliness, hearing, bread, teaching, peace, social inclusion, forgiveness, table fellowship, life—is in some way a precursor to his gift of
himself, of his own accord, as a ransom for many.

His parables, strikingly, reinforce the picture of God as an irre-
pressible giver, even when they are not mainly about God. Once there
was a farmer who scattered seed so liberally that most of it didn't
take root. Once there was a king who gave remittance for a debt of ten
thousand talents. Once there was a vineyard-owner who gave people
far more than their work was worth. Once there was a father who
gave away half his estate to his rebellious son (and then gave him a
feast when he came crawling back, having wasted it all). Once there

---

2 Luke 1:28.
3 Matthew 2:11.
4 John 1:16.

was a nobleman who gave three months' wages to all his employees, and then went on a foreign trip. Once there was a landowner who gave his vineyard over to tenants. Once there was a king who gave wedding invitations to every undesirable in the county. In fact, it is hard to think of a parable in which a God-figure features and he is not characterized by giving away far more than he should.

There is also a certain extravagance, verging on wastefulness, to his miracles. How many weddings have you been to where they need one hundred and fifty gallons of fine wine? Why can't a person who can miraculously multiply bread and fish also count, so as not to end up overcatering by twelve baskets? If you could heal someone with a word, why would you wait until they had been dead for three days before raising them, putrid graveclothes and all, in front of the whole village? What is the point of walking on water rather than swimming, or calming a storm rather than looking at the clouds and muttering something about it being better to go sailing tomorrow? Why does a death need to be accompanied not just by earthquakes, dark skies, and torn curtains, but also by the coming to life of dozens of random people? Who produces 153 fish out of nowhere, to the point that the boat carrying them nearly sinks (and while we're on that story, who was counting them all, and why?)? Who does it twice?

Yet these miracles, generous and gracious as they are, are so eclipsed by the gift of Christ himself that many of us fail to notice them as gifts at all. Despite the last few pages of examples, there is only one thing in Paul's mind when he writes, "Thanks be to God for his inexpressible gift!",[5] and anyone with even a passing knowledge of the Christian tradition knows exactly what it is. Clearly, the apostles regard everything as being given by God. But it is Jesus, crucified and risen, who is the focus of such statements as "the grace of God has appeared,"[6] or "but the free gift is not like the trespass,"[7] or "by grace you have been saved through faith. And this is not your own doing; it

---

5   2 Corinthians 9:15.
6   Titus 2:11.
7   Romans 5:15.

is the gift of God."[8] Every breath, step, meal or vista we have is gift—"What do you have that you did not receive?"[9] —but they recede into insignificance before the Lord Jesus Christ, the Gift himself, like stars fading before the risen sun.

Then comes the Spirit. Jesus spoke about this gift more than any other, bursting with anticipation. Just a little while, and I will come to you. I will ask the Father, and he will give you another Helper to be with you forever. It is to your advantage that I go away, because if I don't, the Helper won't come. I give you my peace. He will lead you into truth. You will receive power. You will witness to me all over the world. Promise, presence, power, proclamation, peace, prophecy, perseverance. Pentecost. From the moment the Spirit is poured out, accompanied by stormy winds and fiery tongues, he is described as a gift, and one on whom Christian experience centers—a gift for all who repent and get baptized, a gift money cannot purchase, a gift now poured out on the gentiles, given to guarantee our eternal inheritance, given to shed abroad the love of God into our hearts, given to make us know, make us feel, that we are children of God. The gifts of the Spirit may be controversial, but the gift of the Spirit is as unifying a doctrine as there is.

And the Spirit is the gift who keeps on giving, throughout the story of the church. He gives us spiritual gifts and spiritual guardians, missionaries and schoolmen, Scriptures and sacraments. He gives us one holy, catholic, and apostolic church, one baptism for the forgiveness of sins, the resurrection of the body, and the life of the world to come. Sometimes his gifts look like successes: the conversion of the Roman empire or the abolition of slavery. Sometimes they look like failures: retreat into the desert or the fragmentation of Europe along religious lines. Sometimes they look spectacular, as revivals or reformations sweep the country. Often they look incredibly ordinary, as peasant farmers and mothers of eight children shuffle into small stone buildings, receive the Word, receive bread and wine, and

---

8 Ephesians 2:8.
9 1 Corinthians 4:7.

shuffle out again. On occasion, you wonder whether his gifts have been withdrawn altogether, as leaders are burned or beheaded and the faithful gather secretly in woodsheds and cellars—but the Spirit keeps giving the peace and truth and stickability we were promised back in the upper room. "And for all this, the church is never spent," you can imagine Hopkins saying. "There lives the dearest freshness deep down things . . . because the Holy Ghost over the bent Church broods, with warm breast and with ah! bright wings."[10]

Finally, the Christian story ends with a new beginning, one that comprises gifts of such excellence and magnitude that even Paul is wary of speculating quite what they will be like. No mind can conceive of it, he says. What you sow doesn't come to life until it dies. Perishable people can't fathom imperishable life. It will be worth it, though; if God didn't spare his own Son, then he's obviously going to give us "all things," isn't he? John is less cautious. It will be like being given the tree of life all over again, being given a white stone with a name that nobody knows, being given authority over the nations, being given white robes, a throne, a crown, an invitation to a wedding feast, a new creation, a river of life, fruit trees, a glorious jewel-festooned city. May the *charis* of the Lord Jesus be with you all. Amen.

Christian theology *is* a theology of gift. We are all, in that sense, charismatics. At the same time, and as a result, most of the discussions, disagreements, and divisions within global Christianity are found within our theology of gift as well. What is central is often controversial.[11]

---

10 Gerard Manley Hopkins, "God's Grandeur," *The Poems of Gerard Manley Hopkins* (London: Oxford, 1967), 66, paraphrased. The original, of course, speaks not of the church but of "nature" and "the bent world."

11 For a magisterial introduction to the way in which different traditions have understood and perfected the concept of gift/grace, from Second Temple Judaism and Greco-Roman philosophy to Jacques Derrida and Pierre Bourdieu, by way of Paul, Augustine, Luther, Kant, Barth, and company, see John Barclay, *Paul and the Gift* (Grand Rapids: Eerdmans, 2015), especially Part I.

So we have Augustine disagreeing with Pelagius over the incongruity of God's grace in salvation. We have Protestants dividing from Roman Catholics over whether the Mass is a gift from God to man or a gift from man to God, and over whether the grace of justification remits all guilt and blots out all punishment (sometimes to the point of burning each other).[12] We have Paedobaptists and Baptists disagreeing over who receives the gift of baptism (sometimes to the point of drowning each other). The Reformed divide from the Lutherans over whether the gifts of bread and wine actually become the real body and blood of Jesus. Wesleyans disagree with Calvinists as to whether grace is irresistible. Pentecostals disagree with cessationists over whether the miraculous gifts of the Spirit continue today. Then there are a multitude of intramural debates over the proper use of gifts like food, drink, sex, pastoral leadership, government, creation, and so on. With the exception of the first and greatest schism in the church's history—which was more a historical and political separation than a theological one—virtually every major dividing line within orthodox Christianity today can be traced back to a disagreement somewhere about the grace, or gifts, of God.

For all this variety, however, the same few questions about gifts recur throughout the church's story. How do we enjoy God's gifts without worshiping them? How do we receive God's gifts without either presuming on them on the one hand or trying to earn them on the other? How, in short, do we respond to the gift? Though the incidentals are continually changing, every generation ends up wrestling with each of these questions somewhere.

Not only that, but each presses itself upon every believer, not just leaders or intellectuals. How to enjoy a gift without worshiping it, which would be idolatry, is a challenge not just for great leaders in church history like Basil or Augustine, but for every ordinary believer

---

12 For this language, see Council of Trent, Session VI, Canon 30: "If anyone says that after the reception of the grace of justification the guilt is so remitted and the debt of eternal punishment so blotted out to every repentant sinner, that no debt of temporal punishment remains to be discharged either in this world or in purgatory before the gates of heaven can be opened, let him be anathema."

who has ever tasted champagne, had sex, or seen the Matterhorn.[13] Similarly, the fitting response to God's gift in salvation—how to receive divine grace without falling into antinomianism (rejection of the law) or legalism—is a consideration for every Christian, not just those confronting Galatian circumcisers, deniers of original sin, indulgence sellers, or cult members.[14] Creation, Christ, the Spirit, the resurrection: these gifts are so large and so unilateral that all of us, however theologically minded we are, have to think through how best to respond to them. "Who has given a gift to him, that he might be repaid? For from him and through him and to him are all things" (Romans 11:35–36).

For respond we must—and always do. Ignoring the gift, or acting as if it had not been given, does not honor the giver. Then again, neither does attempting to earn it or repay it, as if we reciprocated God's purchase of the first round of drinks by offering to buy the next one. No, a Christian response to the gifts of God begins with the acknowledgment that they are good (as opposed to bad or ambiguous), that he is giving them (as opposed to exchanging them or bribing with them), and that we are receiving them (as opposed to reciprocating them or rejecting them). From there, our response comprises at least four things: thankfulness, worship, stewardship, and pursuit.

Thankfulness is two-sided. The obvious reason we encourage children to say thank you, and the obvious reason Paul encourages his churches to be thankful so frequently, is that thankfulness is the fitting response to a gift; it honors the giver and demonstrates that the receiver has reacted appropriately.[15] In Paul's Greek, the words for "gratitude" and "grace" are often the same—"*charis* be to God through Jesus Christ our Lord," for instance, or "singing, with *charis*

13 A good recent treatment of this theme is found in Joe Rigney, *The Things of Earth: Treasuring God by Enjoying His Gifts* (Wheaton: Crossway, 2015).

14 For a helpful, contemporary, and surprising angle on this problem, see Sinclair Ferguson, *The Whole Christ: Legalism, Antinomianism and Gospel Assurance—Why the Marrow Controversy Still Matters* (Wheaton: Crossway, 2015).

15 See the magisterial work of Peter Leithart, *Gratitude: An Intellectual History* (Waco: Baylor, 2014).

in your hearts to God"[16] —so Paul responds to grace in the most suitable way possible, returning *charis* for *charis*. We respond to gifts (***charis****mata*) by giving thanks (*eu**charis**teō*).[17]

There is a human side to it as well, however. When something beautiful happens, as C. S. Lewis pointed out, being thankful for it is part of how we enjoy it: "The delight is incomplete until it is expressed."[18] Thanking God for the aroma of freshly ground coffee enhances our enjoyment of coffee. When our friend buys us tickets to the game, our enjoyment of the gift begins when we hug them with gratitude. This is the second, less obvious reason that Paul exhorts thankfulness in his converts: thanking God for his gifts forces us to ponder what we have rather than what we lack, and to enjoy them all over again, if only for a moment. It displaces foul speech and greed and anxiety and asceticism.[19] It makes envy impossible. It awakens the soul to the realities of God's gifts, and joy follows.

As this happens, we *worship*. We do not merely acknowledge the goodness of the gift, but the goodness of the Giver, reckoning that the sort of God who would create a world in which the sun clocks off every evening in a fanfare of crimson and orange, only to rise the next morning with a similar explosion of color, must himself be intensely

---

16 Colossians 3:16.

17 We should note the significance of the linguistic connection here: it is not just that Eucharist is an act of thanksgiving, but that as Leithart points out, thanksgiving is an act of daily Eucharist. "Giving thanks is a pattern of acknowledgement, recital, memorial, and feast. Or: we give thanks when we take, bless, break, and distribute. How might that translate into a daily Eucharistic liturgy? Acknowledge this thing, experience (good or bad), person as a gift from a loving heavenly Father, from whom are all things. Ask: How can I incorporate this thing, this experience (good or bad), this person into a recital of God's great acts for me and for his people? Ask: How can I memorialize this thing, experience, person? How can it become a 'reminder' to God to be faithful and an aid to my memory? Ask: How can my encounter with this experience, thing, or person become communion with God, an act of covenant renewal? How can this person come to *share* thanksgiving with me? Ask: How can my response to this thing, experience, person be a continuing witness to the goodness, faithfulness, and justice of God? How can my response become an assault on powers and principalities in heavenly places? Ask: How can I receive this thing, experience, person so as to break and distribute it for the nourishment, edification, and joy of others? How can I bring others to share in my thanks?" Peter Leithart, "What Is Thanks? Daily Eucharist," http://www.patheos.com/blogs/leithart/2017/09/thanks-daily-eucharist.

18 C. S. Lewis, *Reflections on the Psalms* (New York: Harcourt, 1958), 95.

19 Ephesians 5:4; Philippians 4:6; 1 Timothy 4:3–4.

glorious and worthy of adoration. We become exegetes of creation. We stand in Yosemite in May, or Provençal fields in August, and infer that the God of bluebells and lavender is creative, generous to a fault, powerful, unpredictable, and lavish. We glimpse divine holiness in thunderstorms, and divine mercy in rainfall. We see the rhythmic, unstoppable consistency of the seasons, year in, year out, and conclude that God is unchangeable, since every good and perfect gift is from above, coming down from the Father of lights with whom there is no variation or shadow due to change. We allow every gift to show us something about the Giver, following the sunbeams back to the sun.[20]

This is how we avoid idolatry. Gifts always present us with the temptation to worship them—stars, crops, sex, animals, even laws—and the best way to fight this temptation is not to abstain from the gifts altogether, but to use them as tools to help us worship God. Augustine, probably the greatest theologian of gift the church has ever seen, wrote about this repeatedly. He distinguished between enjoying something for its own sake (*frui*), which is how we should enjoy God, and making use of something to enjoy something higher than itself (*uti*), which is how we should enjoy created things. Gifts, he said, are like vessels that carry us back to our homeland; they should be enjoyed, but only in that they are taking us to our true source of joy and our true love.[21] So, he argued, "if the things of this world delight you, praise God for them, but turn your love away from them and give it to their Maker."[22] Give thanks, in other words, but turn your gratitude into worship. "For he loves you too little, who loves anything along with you, which he loves not for your sake."[23]

Thirdly, we are called to *stewardship*. This, of the four responses, is the one that Jesus focuses on the most in his parables: invest your minas, cultivate your vineyard, use your wealth to make friends,

---

20 The image is from C. S. Lewis, "Meditation in a Toolshed," in *God in the Dock: Essays on Theology and Ethics* (Grand Rapids: Eerdmans, 1970), 212–15.
21 Augustine, *De Doctrina Christiana*, 1:3–4.
22 Augustine, *Confessions*, 4:12.
23 Augustine, *Confessions*, 10:29.

make the most of your talents, trim your lamps, and if you don't, don't be surprised if you lose the whole lot. Gifts cannot be earned, but they can be spurned. Make the most of what you have, and more will be added.

It may be materialism, or it may be something else entirely, but if you mention the word *stewardship*, the chances are that many in the contemporary Western church—and certainly those who have been into a bookshop or heard a sermon series—will assume it refers to gifts of common grace: money, time, relationships, the world. Steward your money with wisdom and generosity. Enhance your abilities with diligence and humility. Take care of creation. Invest in your marriage. Manage your time wisely. Paperbacks do not proliferate quite so much, however, on our stewardship of special grace: spiritual gifts, the sacraments, the gospel itself. The apostles go there regularly. "As each has received a gift, use it to serve one another, as good stewards of God's varied grace" (1 Peter 4:10). "Having gifts that differ according to the grace given to us, let us use them" (Romans 12:6). "This is how one should regard us, as servants of Christ and stewards of the mysteries of God" (1 Corinthians 4:1). "By the grace of God I am what I am, and his grace toward me was not in vain. On the contrary, I worked harder than any of them, though it was not I, but the grace of God that is with me" (1 Corinthians 15:10). Grace works. Every gift from God is an opportunity for stewardship.

The fourth response to divine gifts, and one which does not contradict but rather supplements the others, is *pursuit*. We react to the gifts we have been given by pursuing more and more of them. We respond to grace by asking for more grace.[24] This seems counterintuitive: we might expect that thankfulness for a past gift was incompatible with pursuit of a future one, or even that pursuing a gift was tantamount to trying to earn it. If, having received a generous wedding gift from my godfather, I immediately set about trying to secure another one, it would seem inappropriate at best,

---

24 The classic contemporary study of this theme is John Piper, *Future Grace: The Purifying Power of the Promises of God* (Colorado Springs: Multnomah, 1995).

manipulative at worst. But that is because something is true of my godfather that is not true of my Father God: his supply is exhaustible. It will run out. When he gives me something, it means he has less for himself or for others. None of these things are true of the one who owns the cattle on a thousand hills and feeds five thousand with a lunch box. Divine gifts are not a zero-sum game.

So we pursue them, and zealously so. Jesus put a daily gift request slap bang in the middle of the Lord's Prayer. His teaching elsewhere implies, even insists, that we should be motivated by future gifts when responding to present ones: "To the one who has, more will be given," "Give, and it will be given to you," and the like. Paul tells the Corinthians that their financial generosity will bring an abundance of grace. He exhorts them to eagerly desire spiritual gifts. James urges us to pursue humility on the grounds that God will always give us more grace if we do. Peter tells believers to grow in grace. It is hard to escape the conclusion that, for Jesus and the apostles, seeking future gifts/grace was an appropriate, and indeed necessary, response to past gifts/grace. What else is petitionary prayer?

Thanksgiving, worship, stewardship, and pursuit: this is how we respond to divine gifts, whether to creation, the gospel, our possessions, our abilities, the sacraments, spiritual gifts, or anything else God has given. "As for the rich," explains Paul in 1 Timothy 6:17–19, "charge them not to be haughty, nor to set their hopes on the uncertainty of riches, but on God [= worship], who richly provides us with everything to enjoy [= thanksgiving]. They are to do good, to be rich in good works, to be generous and ready to share [= stewardship], thus storing up treasure for themselves as a good foundation for the future, so that they may take hold of that which is truly life [= pursuit]." The four belong together.

God is continually giving gifts to his people. Whenever he does, the most appropriate response on our part is to thank him for them, worship him through them, make good use of them, and seek more of them—and in doing so, we will avoid earning them, spurning them, or idolizing them. So far, so good. What does this mean for our corporate worship?

It means this: that the church will mature and flourish to the extent that she makes use of all of the gifts God has given her. If things are given by God for use in corporate worship—songs and psalms, prayers and creeds, prophecies and languages, Scriptures and sermons, bread and wine, oil and water—then we should receive them with thankfulness, praise God through them, look after them carefully, and pursue them. Gifts make us larger, richer, stronger. Marginalizing a particular divine gift because it does not fit with our denominational tradition, if it is indeed a divine gift, should not be an option.

In the charismatic tradition, for instance, it is common to jettison any historic practice that looks "religious"—the vagueness of this key term is significant—including creeds, set prayers, the reading of the Law (unless it immediately precedes a sermon, of course), corporate confession, words of assurance, the benediction, and in some cases even the Lord's Supper. All of these, as "formal" or "ritual" activities, lack spontaneity, which means they lack authenticity, which means they lack spirituality.[25] Consequently they are generally avoided, for fear of cluttering up the program with anything that isn't singing, preaching, or notices.

Fortunately, the more established, historically rooted churches would never do anything so unwise. They would only jettison practices that reinforce a shallow, hyped, inane, happy-clappy, gnostic, experience-obsessed spirituality. Unfortunately, in practice, this often translates into the avoidance of most of the physical responses we find in the Psalms (dancing, shouting, falling facedown, raising hands, playing loud cymbals), and most of the spiritual gifts we find in Paul (prophecy, healing, faith, miracles, distinguishing between spirits, words of knowledge, words of wisdom, languages, interpreting

---

25 There are echoes here of Charles Taylor's discussion of "the age of authenticity" in his *A Secular Age* (Cambridge: Harvard University Press, 2007), chapter 13.

languages)—as well as anything that might indicate that God is at work spontaneously or that Jesus has actually defeated the devil or that the Holy Spirit is shedding God's love abroad and crying "Abba!" from deep within us. Thus we avoid asinine flippancy and replace it with frumpy austerity. Out of the frying pan, into the fire.

These are caricatures, clearly. But they may serve to show what happens when certain gifts, given by God for his people to use in corporate worship, are overlooked by the church, whether in passive neglect or active rejection. A robust theology of gift will steer us away from hitting the rocks on either side, and encourage us not just to allow both eucharistic and charismatic gifts, but to celebrate them, treasure them, and pursue them. If, as Paul puts it, God's various gifts are given "for the common good" and "for the building up of the church," then we should expect to flourish to the extent that we receive, steward, and enjoy them.[26]

The gods of the nations offer ambiguous gifts, but the God of Israel does not. As he demonstrates from the first page of Scripture to the last, and most emphatically in the Lord Jesus Christ, his grace gifts are always given to bless, to rescue, to delight. If we know that a particular practice has been given to us by God, then we already know something vital about its nature. We know that whatever we might instinctively think about it—or whatever our prior experiences of it may have been—it will always be very, very good.

---

26 1 Corinthians 12:7; 14:12; etc.

CHAPTER 3

CHARA

Joy Unspeakable

Christians have joy unspeakable, full of glory, but you might not always know it to look at us.

In many church traditions, especially Western ones, we find it easier to lament than to rejoice. We have a commendable desire to be serious about the things of God, but our history suggests there is a slippery slope from seriousness, to sobriety, to solemnity, to sadness. Fasting through Lent is commonplace; feasting through Eastertide is rare. Most secular people think the odds of laughing in a church are about as great as the odds of laughing at the puns on their notice boards. We have a *Via Dolorosa*, or Way of Sorrows, but despite the fact that Jesus scorned the shame of crucifixion "for the joy set before him," no *Via Laetitia*, or Way of Joy.[1] Many still pray as "miserable" sinners, despite the word's change in meaning from "wretched, in need of mercy" to "unhappy, gloomy." It can be self-fulfilling.

Our art and music represent Jesus as sad and suffering far more than as triumphant and risen. More than a few cathedrals and churches would suggest to an uninitiated visitor that the hero

---

1 Hebrews 12:2 NIV.

of all those stained glass windows and sculptures, inscriptions and crypts, was tragically dead rather than gloriously alive. (When the risen Christ is represented at all—and I'm not saying he should be, but that's another story—he is usually lifting his hands in front of him and gazing to heaven, which looks to modern people like he is shrugging his shoulders and giving the disciples an eye-roll, and that doesn't help either.) Depictions of hell, from Dante to Botticelli, are often far more vivid than depictions of heaven.

Even in our moments of high celebration, the minor key pops up in the most unexpected places, including numerous *Magnificats* ("My soul magnifies the Lord and my spirit rejoices in God my Saviour") and Easter hymns ("Let the Church with gladness hymns of triumph sing," with the word "sing" receiving the lowest and gloomiest chord of all), serving as an accidental parody of our struggle to be unequivocally happy about something. The happiest songs can lose their edge through something as mundane as punctuation, as a call to uproarious merriment at Christmas ("God rest ye merry, gentlemen!") becomes a prayer for the happy guys to sit on the sofa and take it easy ("God rest ye, merry gentlemen"). Our most recognizable symbol is the cross, or the crucifix, rather than the circle of moved stone and empty tomb. It is as if the Western church has been playing a very one-sided game of tic-tac-toe.

Some strands of contemporary Christianity, put off by this air of melancholy, have swung to the opposite extreme. Consumer-friendly churches can attract people with a spirituality in which there is no room for sorrow whatsoever. Suffering is regarded as an aberration. Immediate solutions are prized—physical, financial, psychological, spiritual—with faithful waiting seen as decidedly second best. Long-term sick people are treated with a mixture of bafflement and impatience. Fasting is the preserve of a few unusually passionate individuals. There is little space for Lent, lament, or Lamentations. Funerals are given the boot and replaced with Celebrations or Services of Thanksgiving. The book of Psalms is trimmed until only the celebratory psalms are left. Hymns that reflect on the sufferings of Christ are replaced by anthemic (and often anemic) crowd-pleasers that, if they make space for grief at all, do so in two cross-centered lines in the penultimate verse before the rhythm section kicks in. Sermons promise a trouble-free lifestyle that would be unattainable, if not incomprehensible, to most Christians in history. Silence may not be kept.

What is fascinating, and strangely encouraging, about all this is that both of these (admittedly cartoonish) traditions go against the grain of Christianity. The normal condition of the Christian life, as the apostle Peter explains, is one of inexpressible and glorious joy, in spite of the fact that we are also grieved by many kinds of trials.[2] We do not ignore the realities of sadness and suffering, but we stubbornly proclaim that they do not have the last word; the kingdom is here, Good Friday ushers in Easter Sunday, and death is swallowed up by life. This, from the resurrection onward, has given Christians a paradoxical way of responding to the brokenness of the world. So Paul and Silas spend a night in the stocks, in an age when that meant muscular agony rather than damp sponges, and hymns reverberate through the cells until an earthquake destroys the prison. Eighteen centuries later, in the same spirit, African slaves stand enchained in cotton fields and sugar plantations, singing the songs of Zion until deliverance comes. Christianity stares death in the face and sings anyway. We are, in Paul's terms, sorrowful yet always rejoicing.

This is modeled on Jesus. He is the one the apostles got it from. No passage in Scripture describes the passion of Christ more powerfully than Isaiah 53:3–4: "A man of sorrows, and acquainted with grief.... Surely he has borne our griefs and carried our sorrows." What is less often noticed is that the passage builds toward a declaration of triumph—"out of the anguish of his soul he shall see and be satisfied" (v. 11)—and that it is sandwiched between outbursts of celebration from Jerusalem's watchmen ("They lift up their voice; together they sing for joy"[3]), Israel as a nation ("Sing, O barren one!"[4]), and creation itself ("The mountains and the hills before you shall break forth into

---

2 1 Peter 1:6–9.
3 Isaiah 52:8.
4 Isaiah 54:1.

singing, and all the trees of the field shall clap their hands"[5]). Hebrews 12:2, no doubt mindful of Isaiah's words, says that Jesus went to the cross in pursuit of joy. *Via Laetitia*, indeed.

When we pan back and consider his life as a whole, it only becomes clearer. The Son of Man grew up in an occupied territory and encountered more injustice, brokenness, demonic oppression, psychological disorder, sickness, sorrow, leprosy, and death in three years than any modern Westerner may in a lifetime. He got exhausted and sad and angry. He wept. Yet when we consider the mood of the Jesus we meet in the Gospels, he seems—and I think this is the right word for it—*jolly*. He loves eating and drinking. He walks with a spring in his step and teaches people between mouthfuls. He is witty. He loves the ridiculous: planks and specks, camels and needles, whitewashed tombs, the blind leading the blind. He draws crowds. He is always sitting at the fun table, so much so that his enemies accuse him (in words that we know the gospel writers would never make up) of being a drunkard and a glutton. That tells us something. God is happier than people think he ought to be in the circumstances.

We get that impression from his parables too. God is like a shepherd who loses something, then finds it again, then invites everyone he knows to rejoice with him. (As in: like no shepherd, ever.) Or like a woman who loses a coin, then finds it, then invites the village round for cocktails to celebrate. (Like no woman, ever.) Or like a father whose disgraced son returns, destitute, putrid, and smelling of pigs, and hares down the lane to hug him and kiss him and invite him to party like it's 1999. Luke uses the word *celebrate* four times in just a few verses, in case we've missed the point.

It may just be me, but I even detect an impish grin, a twinkle in the eye, when he is debating with people who are plotting to kill him. Where's your authority? say the bumptious officials with headsets and luminous yellow jackets. Show me yours and I'll show you mine, he says. Whose wife will this woman be in the resurrection? Go and read the Bible, dummy. Taxes or no taxes? Look at this image, and

---

5 Isaiah 55:12.

give him what he deserves. How dare you claim to forgive sins? Well I was going to make this man walk again, but thought it might be too easy. The last time we see Jesus in the four gospels, he is chatting with his friends at a barbecue on the beach, and that seems strangely appropriate. Sorrowful at times, yes. Yet always rejoicing.

Given his example, it is hardly surprising that Christians have, at our best, both cried more and laughed more than anyone else, but with the accent on the latter. Few people have seen the connection as clearly as G. K. Chesterton in the final two paragraphs of *Orthodoxy*:

> Man is more himself when joy is the fundamental thing in him, and grief the superficial. Melancholy should be an innocent interlude, a tender and fugitive frame of mind; praise should be the permanent pulsation of the soul. . . .
>
> The tremendous figure which fills the Gospels towers in this respect, as in every other, above all the thinkers who ever thought themselves tall. . . . There was some one thing that he covered constantly by abrupt silence or impetuous isolation when he walked upon our earth; and I have sometimes fancied that it was his mirth.[6]

So when we act as those who are rejoicing yet always sorrowful, rather than sorrowful yet always rejoicing, we are swimming against the stream: of history, of Scripture, of Christ himself. "It is a Christian duty, as you know," wrote C. S. Lewis to a friend, "for everyone to be as happy as he can."[7] This is the day that Yahweh has made; let us rejoice and be glad in it! At your right hand are pleasures forever! Rejoice in the Lord always, and again I say, rejoice! The chief end of man, as the Westminster catechism has it, is to glorify God—and enjoy him forever.

---

6 G. K. Chesterton, *Orthodoxy*, in *The Wit, Whimsy, and Wisdom of G. K. Chesterton* (Landisville: Coachwhip, 2009), 312.

7 Quoted in Sheldon Vanauken, *A Severe Mercy* (New York: HarperCollins, 1980), 189.

In a public ministry that lasted around three years, the apostle John tells us, Jesus did enough things to fill the world with books. Many of them defied the imagination. But the first "sign" that manifested his glory, and caused his disciples to believe in him, was quite literally a party piece. He went to a wedding and turned one hundred and fifty gallons of water into fine wine.

That raises the obvious question: Why? Why—having resolved to take on flesh at this particular point in history, having waited for thousands of years to do so—did the Son of God decide that his first sign would be something so apparently unnecessary? This is not a story about the poor being fed, the sick being healed, or the oppressed being set free. It doesn't reveal the compassion of God like an exorcism does, or the power of God like walking on the water. If anything, it could look like an endorsement of undercatering. Or stinginess. Or drunkenness. It could prompt subsequent generations of Christians to drink to excess (which many have) or to spend money on luxuries that are surplus to requirements (which many have) or to recognize the dangers of such things and ban alcohol altogether (which many have).[8] Yet Jesus made this, rather than raising a dead girl or calming a storm, the first "sign" that manifested his glory. It is curious, to say the least.

Much of our curiosity stems from the fact that we have lost the rich biblical symbolism of wine. It is not primarily that most Protestant churches now substitute grape juice for Communion wine—which can be defended, whether or not we agree with it—but that, in doing so, we do not recognize that we have lost anything. Wine is just a red drink, right? Grape juice looks just as blood-like as Merlot. What's the problem? In the scriptural imagination, however, and particularly in the prophetic tradition, wine represents abundance, *shalom*, hope, and new creation. It embodies blessing ("May God give you of the dew of heaven and of the fatness of the earth and plenty of grain and wine!") and happiness ("wine to gladden the heart

---

8 It is hard to resist mentioning that, when I asked this question on Twitter—"What does it say about a guy if his first sign is winemaking?"—my friend Sam Allberry simply replied: "That he probably isn't a Southern Baptist?"

of man, oil to make his face shine and bread to strengthen man's heart").[9] It speaks of love ("we will extol your love more than wine") and bounty ("then your barns will be filled with plenty, and your vats will be bursting with wine").[10]

Since vineyards take such a long time to grow, their presence is associated with peace and stability. For a nation that has been marched through once every forty-four years for the last four millennia, Isaiah's promise that "they shall build houses and inhabit them; they shall plant vineyards and eat their fruit" reverberates with the promise of a more harmonious future.[11] Grapes also suggest the promise of an inheritance: it is not a coincidence that the Israelite spies came back with giant bunches of grapes, nor that they named the valley *Eshcol*, "cluster," after it.[12] To this day, otherwise obscure valleys and villages around the world are known for the grapes they produce—Medoc, Napa Valley, Barolo, Sauternes—and for their evocative power that entices travelers to return. Wines, more than anything else the earth produces, capture a unique sense of place, such that the French even have their own word, *terroir*, for the specific piece of land from which a wine comes. The grapes of Pomerol say to us what the grapes of Eshcol said to Israel: come back—soon—to this land of plenty and beauty. Grapes carry promise.

Wine is served at weddings and feasts and other occasions of joy. As such, it points forward to the resurrection, when "the LORD of hosts will make for all peoples a feast of rich food, a feast of well-aged wine, of rich food full of marrow, of aged wine well refined" (Isaiah 25:6). When the presence of God is withdrawn, on the other hand, wine disappears, along with all traces of music and happiness: "The wine mourns, the vine languishes, all the merry-hearted sigh. The mirth of the tambourines is stilled, the noise of the jubilant has ceased" (Isaiah 24:7–8). Nevertheless, Israel's hope is that God will

---

9 Genesis 27:28; Psalm 104:15.
10 Song of Solomon 1:4; Proverbs 3:10.
11 Isaiah 65:21; for the statistic, see N. T. Wright, *The New Testament and the People of God* (London: SPCK, 1992), 3.
12 Numbers 13:23–24.

one day restore them, and restore creation itself, so that "the mountains shall drip sweet wine, and all the hills shall flow with it" (Amos 9:13). Joy will conquer sorrow, and salvation will conquer judgment. When God judged the old creation, it was covered in water. When he resurrects the new one, it will be covered in wine.

Which takes us back to Cana. The transformation of water into wine is far more than a demonstration that Jesus loves weddings, although he does; it is a sign that joy and abundance and restoration, and even glory, are now here, breaking into a world for the first time in the person of Jesus. It is a physical expression of his enigmatic saying in the other Gospels: new wine has arrived, and the old wineskins will not be able to cope with it. The banquet that Isaiah promised is nearly upon us. The bridegroom is here, and the champagne corks are being popped. Old creation water is being displaced by new creation wine. Weeping may tarry for the night. But joy cometh in the morning.

Given all this imagery, both in the prophets and the Gospels, we might expect wine to be mentioned throughout Acts and the New Testament letters. In fact, it is hardly mentioned at all. There are a few comments about using the drink wisely (some warnings about drinking too much, or causing others to drink too much, and a reference to using it as a medicine), but other than that, wine only crops up in two contexts.[13] These two contexts, however, are highly significant for our daily search for joy and for this book as a whole. We find wine mentioned when people talk about the Lord's Supper and when they talk about the filling with the Holy Spirit.

In the Eucharist, in anticipation of the day we will drink once again with our bridegroom in his Father's kingdom, the church drinks wine. On the day of Pentecost, the church looks as if it has been drinking wine, even though it hasn't. Sincere and well-motivated efforts have been made to remove the alcohol from texts like these, but since drunkenness was a problem at the Corinthian Communion table, and since Peter defended the church against the charge of

---

13 Instructions to use the drink wisely: Romans 14:21; 1 Timothy 3:8; 5:23; Titus 2:3.

being "filled with new wine" by insisting that "these people are not drunk, as you suppose," commentators have rightly recognized that it belongs.[14] Incidentally, the fact that Paul urges us to be "filled with the Spirit" as opposed to being "drunk with wine" suggests that this association is not random mockery, thrown from the cheap seats for the sake of discrediting the believers, but has some basis in reality. With all the proper caveats about excess and addiction in place, there is clearly *something* about being filled with the Spirit that is analogous to being filled with wine. Both experiences prompt people to rejoice, sing, and make music.[15] Both experiences take us out of ourselves, so to speak.[16] Both experiences, as Martyn Lloyd-Jones famously put it, can be described as being "under the influence."[17]

This is remarkable. Wine, the prophetic symbol of joy and abundance and new creation, features in the ongoing life of the church in two ways: as a physical representation of Christ's presence in the Eucharist and as a metaphorical representation of the Spirit's presence since Pentecost. Like wine, both the sacraments and the Spirit bring joy. Like wine, they lead the church into anticipation and thankfulness, celebration and song. Like wine, they witness to the new creation that is coming, offering us a glass from the early harvest now while we wait for the full vintage to be bottled in late summer. The early church, we could almost say, was oenologically Eucharismatic.

Almost, but not quite.

On the one hand, it should be fairly clear that the gifts of bread, wine, and water have been given to the church for our joy, among

---

14 1 Corinthians 11:21; Acts 2:13–15.

15 Ephesians 5:18–19.

16 See Jaroslav Pelikan, *Acts* (Grand Rapids: Brazos, 2005), 50: "It is right to want to be 'filled' with something, and the drunkard quite properly recognizes that human nature stands in need of some power that will take it out of itself (as alcohol and drugs do). But this need also includes the requirement that such fullness will in the process not corrupt and destroy it (as alcohol also does), but fulfill it."

17 Martyn Lloyd-Jones, *Life in the Spirit: An Exposition of Ephesians 5:18–6:9* (Edinburgh: Banner of Truth, 1974), 48.

other things, and that our happiness would be diminished dramatically if we were to neglect any of them. The Passover was a feast and the Last Supper was a Passover, so there was a celebratory, festival quality to the Lord's Supper from the beginning, as God's people gathered to remember and rejoice in their deliverance from slavery. The first time we hear about the church breaking bread together, we are told that they did so in their homes "with glad and generous hearts." Paul spoke of the "cup of blessing." Jude referred to "love feasts."[18] Baptism, likewise, is frequently associated with rejoicing in the book of Acts, as Samaritan cities, Ethiopian eunuchs, and Philippian jailers receive baptism and go on their way rejoicing.[19] The church, like Israel, goes down into the waters as they flee from their enemy—and the church, like Israel, comes up again to discover that her enemy has been defeated, which it immediately celebrates with a song and a dance.[20] Sacraments fuel happiness.

The same is true, only more so, for the Holy Spirit. To be filled with the Spirit is to be filled with joy. When Jesus promises the Helper to his disciples, he cannot stop talking about how their joy will be full.[21] Luke remarks that the disciples in Antioch "were filled with joy and with the Holy Spirit," and Paul reminds the Thessalonians that they "received the word in much affliction, with the joy of the Holy Spirit."[22] The fruit of the Spirit is joy. The kingdom of God is a matter of joy in the Holy Spirit. God's love has been poured into our hearts through the Holy Spirit who has been given to us, and for that reason we rejoice in the hope of the glory of God.[23] That's why Paul's command to "be filled with the Spirit" is explicated in such happy ways: singing, making melody, thanking, and submitting to each other. Jesus "rejoiced in the Holy Spirit," and so do we.[24]

On the other hand, this is not the same as saying that, to be truly

---

18 Acts 2:46; 1 Corinthians 10:16; Jude 12.
19 Acts 8:8, 12, 36–39; 16:33–34.
20 See Exodus 14–15.
21 John 14–16.
22 Acts 13:52; 1 Thessalonians 1:6.
23 Galatians 5:22; Romans 14:17; 5:2–5.
24 Luke 10:21 NIV; Ephesians 5:18.

joyful, the church needs to be "Eucharismatic" in the way I am painting it in this book: sacramentally deep, historically rooted, liturgically rich, miraculously inclined, charismatically zealous, visibly celebratory. Thousands of churches do their utmost to stress that baptism doesn't "do" anything and Communion is "just a symbol," and God blesses them with his presence just the same. Millions of believers experience the joy of the Spirit without ever shouting about it, dancing about it, or believing that the miraculous gifts are available today. In the context of this book, it is important to be crystal clear on that. If we are in Christ, then the joy of the Lord is our strength, whether our corporate gatherings are Eucharismatic or not.

Having said that, it really helps if they are. A biblical and historical defense of this claim will have to wait for the following chapters, but in the meantime, three observations will suffice.

The first is an observation about our emotional lives, namely that going higher requires going deeper, and vice versa. Many (if not most) Christians today would be inclined to think in terms of a spectrum when it comes to church practice, with the historical-liturgical-reflective-sacramental at one end, and the charismatic-Pentecostal-expressive-celebratory at the other. For a whole of host of historical reasons, which we do not have time to trace here, these two forms of worship often appear to be in tension with one another; if you want depth, come this way, and if you want bounce, go that way.[25] The truth, however, is quite the opposite. If you want more bounce, you need more depth. Ask any trampolinist. Or tree, for that matter.

Without depth, height is unsustainable. Inspirational messages, emotive music, anemic liturgy, and cathartic experiences can only take us so far; whether or not they produce a short-term emotional response, they cannot build the kind of faith that, like Habakkuk, rejoices in God even when there is no fruit on the vine or herds in the

---

25 A short history of this apparent spectrum would have to include the impact of Montanism, iconoclasm, late medieval heresy, Anabaptism, Methodism, nineteenth-century revivalism, and racial segregation in the US—which would presumably make it a longish history.

stalls.[26] For that, as the black church always has, we may need to borrow some resilient joy from our ancestors. Rather than attempting standing jumps in the center of the trampoline, which is exhausting as well as ineffective, we need to plunge ourselves into the depths of our tradition, so as to spring to new heights. Down, into historic prayers. Up, into spontaneous ones. Down, into confession of sin. Up, into celebration of forgiveness. Down, into the creeds. Up, into the choruses. Down, into knowing God's presence in the sacraments. Up, into feeling God's presence in song. Call, and response. Friday, then Sunday. Kneel, then jump.

This metaphor cuts both ways. Going deeper also requires going higher. We are embodied and emotional creatures, and a person who dances for joy, as opposed to merely singing about it, is more likely to be a person who falls on their face, as opposed to leaning forward and putting their head between their knees for a few seconds. (This both/and is precisely what we see in Leviticus, when fire comes out from the presence of the Lord as the priesthood is consecrated: "And when all the people saw it, they shouted for joy and fell facedown.")[27] Those who laugh in church are more likely to cry there. If you are captivated by the presence and gifts of the Spirit in worship, you will probably find the presence and gifts of the Spirit in the sacraments more wonderful, not less. If you go further up, you go further in.

The second observation is that this is also the dynamic we encounter in the Psalms. Surely no text in history combines such rich, poetic, and searching liturgy with such exuberant noise. Every time I open my Bible at random and find it falls open in the book of Psalms, it serves as a gentle reminder that God wanted a big book of prayerful liturgy to be at the center of our lives—and that the liturgy he had in mind was to be an emotional and doxological roller coaster, whose heights were higher, and depths deeper, than anywhere else in literature.

---

26 Habakkuk 3:17–19.
27 Leviticus 9:24 (NIV).

I have spent much of my life in charismatic or Pentecostal churches, but I have never attended one more celebratory than the book of Psalms. Sing praises! Sing a new song! Clap your hands, all you nations! Wake up, my soul; awake, O harp and lyre, and I will awaken the dawn! Come, let us sing for joy to the Lord; let us shout aloud to the Rock of our salvation! With trumpets and the sound of the horn, make a joyful noise! Lift up your hands to the holy place and bless the Lord! Let them praise his name with dancing, making melody with tambourine and lyre! Praise him with loud clashing cymbals![28] Nor can we dismiss this party atmosphere as hyperbolic, as if these calls to noisy celebration are the sorts of things songwriters say when they get carried away, but nobody would think of actually doing. David, who wrote quite a few of them, danced before the Lord so vigorously that he embarrassed his wife. When the wall of Jerusalem was dedicated under Nehemiah, "the sound of rejoicing could be heard far away."[29] Given the explicit instructions of the Psalms, and the fact that Christians are urged to sing and teach one another with them, it is even worth asking whether churches that never play loud music, sing new songs, clap, raise hands, shout, or dance are not just reserved or conservative but actually unbiblical.[30]

Yet the Psalms know depths as well as heights, and in many ways more so. In fact, virtually every element that has featured historically in eucharistic and liturgical worship can be found in them.[31]

---

28 Psalm 9:11; 33:3; 47:1; 57:8; 95:1; 98:6; 134:2; 149:3; 150:5.

29 Nehemiah 12:43.

30 Advocates of the Regulative Principle might point out that none of these instructions are explicitly restated in the New Testament, but the fact that we are urged to sing, teach with, and admonish each other with the Psalms (Ephesians 5:19; Colossians 3:16) suggests that, implicitly at least, they are. Clearly there are imperatives in the Psalms that Christians are not intended to obey—"execute vengeance on the nations and punishments on the peoples," for instance (Psalm 149:7)—but this is clear in the pages of the New Testament and has been since the start of the church. By contrast, it is difficult to imagine the (Jewish) early church ignoring the calls to noisy exultation in the Psalter from Pentecost onward, and equally difficult to imagine the church in Ephesus singing Psalm 150 while decrying the use of dancing or musical instruments in worship.

31 Interestingly, another biblical book that contains almost all the elements of subsequent Christian liturgy is Revelation—prayer, prophecy, exhortation, songs of praise and worship, reading of letters, incense, lament, proclamation of the gospel, the exposition of a scroll, lament, doxology, benediction, bread and wine, intercession, silence, bowing down, a wedding feast, and so

Set prayers for specific occasions (70). Confession (51). Words of assurance (23; 91). Repetition (like the "chorus" of 42–43, or the call-and-response of 136). Extended meditations on Scripture or the cross (119; 22). Lament (most darkly, 88). Praise (146–50). Anointing with oil (23:5; 45:7; 89:20; 92:10). Intercession for rulers and nations, or for the sick (72; 35). Creeds (103).[32] Liturgical storytelling that memorializes God's saving work amongst the people, usually focused on the story of Passover and Exodus (78; in Christian terms, this is effectively a sacramental liturgy).[33] Kneeling and bowing down (95:6; 138:2). Worship according to an annual calendar (120–34). Cries for justice and deliverance (10; 38; 137). Songs of teaching and wisdom (37). Benediction (67). Silence (4:4; 46:10).[34]

When we consider the liturgical breadth of the Psalms, many contemporary churches look pretty insipid in comparison. Some of us limit ourselves to the songs of triumph and avoid laments like the plague, while others prefer the dirge to the dance; as Dorothy Parker impishly said of Katharine Hepburn, we run the full gamut of emotions from A to B. The Psalms, like Scripture as a whole, call us to a richer, more rounded, more honest pursuit of joy, in which there is merriment and gravitas, treble and bass. It is also one in which our physical postures—bowing, kneeling, weeping, falling silent, dancing, shouting, clapping, raising hands, making melody—not only reflect, but also facilitate, our worship in Spirit and in truth.[35]

---

on—and John begins by telling us he is "in the Spirit on the Lord's Day" (1:10). Cf. the comment of Peter Leithart, *Revelation 1–11* (London: Bloomsbury T&T Clark, 2018), 345: "On Sunday, after we have confessed sin in response to an exhortation, we are absolved and ascend in song to the presence of God, and when we get to the throne, where the Word of God will be read, we fall silent and let the trumpet-voiced reader of the Scriptures speak God's trumpet-word to us, so the prophet who has eaten the book can speak what he has consumed."

32 The Puritan Edward Reynolds also referred to Psalm 110 as "*symbolum Davidicum*, the prophet David's creed," arguing that all items of the Apostles' Creed were essentially contained within it; see *The Whole Works of the Right Reverend Edward Reynolds* (London: Holdsworth, 1826), 2:7.

33 For an exploration of the sacramental significance of the exodus story, see Alastair J. Roberts and Andrew Wilson, *Echoes of Exodus: Tracing Themes of Redemption through Scripture* (Wheaton, Ill.: Crossway, 2018).

34 It is possible, though not certain, that the *Selahs* were also used in this way.

35 It is common to think of bodily postures as responses to emotional states (so we dance if we are happy, kneel if we feel reverent, shout if we are impassioned, and so on), but from a biblical perspective this is unfounded; if anything, our emotions respond to our postures. Cf. C. S. Lewis,

The third observation is more historical: the story of the church suggests that believers have always had profound experiences of joy in both eucharistic and charismatic ways. The eucharistic side of that is not particularly surprising, given the centrality of the Lord's Supper (or the Mass) in both the Eastern Orthodox and Roman Catholic traditions. Modern evangelicals, sometimes inclined to see the medieval church as a black hole of spiritual darkness, would do well to read the devotional writings of Bernard of Clairvaux, Thomas Aquinas, Hildegard of Bingen, Thomas à Kempis, and company. No matter how Protestant we are, we cannot escape the fact that the Eucharist was the chief way in which our brothers and sisters encountered divine joy and intimacy with Christ for over a thousand years.

More surprising, but no less real, is the charismatic dimension of historic spirituality. To take one famous example, nobody who has read Blaise Pascal's memorial is likely to forget it:

Monday, 23 November, feast of St. Clement, pope and martyr, and others in the martyrology. Vigil of St. Chrysogonus, martyr, and others. From about half past ten at night until about half past midnight, FIRE.

GOD of Abraham, GOD of Isaac, GOD of Jacob—not of the philosophers and of the learned. Certitude. Certitude. Feeling. Joy. Peace.

GOD of Jesus Christ. My God and your God. Your GOD will be my God. Forgetfulness of the world and of everything, except GOD. He is only found by the ways taught in the Gospel. Grandeur of the human soul.

Righteous Father, the world has not known you, but I have known you. Joy, joy, joy, tears of joy.

It does not especially matter whether we refer to such a testimony with biblical language like "baptism in the Spirit" or "filling with the

---

The Screwtape Letters (London: Collins, 2016), 16: "At the very least, they can be persuaded that the bodily position makes no difference to their prayers; for they constantly forget, what you must always remember, that they are animals and that what their bodies do affects their souls."

Spirit," or whether we prefer vaguer terms like "mystical experience"; it is the reality, which has all sorts of parallels across the centuries (and particularly in times of awakening or revival), that counts.[36] Even more famous, but less often recognized as an example of charismatic experience, is Augustine's conversion story in the *Confessions*. In the space of a few pages, he tells of how he shakes with emotion, hears God speak to him, bursts into tears, hears the voice of a child that he interprets "as a command to me from heaven," opens Scripture at random, reads Romans 13:13–14, and is converted—experiences that will be familiar to charismatics the world over but might make more cautious readers a bit nervous.[37] If we broaden out into his *City of God*, we will find a whole chapter devoted to the ongoing reality of miracles, prophetic dreams, and healings. As he puts it at the end of describing one of them: "No words of mine can describe the joy, and praise, and thanksgiving to the merciful and almighty God which was poured from the lips of all, with tears of gladness. Let the scene be imagined rather than described!"[38] As Peter said: joy unspeakable.

To personalize this for a moment: in the first ten years of my Christian life, I remember two experiences of joy that outstripped all others. One of them was as charismatic as they come—at a huge meeting at a Bible week, on a campsite, falling facedown on the floor in awe as a spontaneous contribution was brought, people cried out in prayer, and a band played "River of God." The other, materially speaking, was the exact opposite—evensong in the chapel of Christ's College, Cambridge, listening to and reflecting on the "Agnus Dei," in Latin, to the melody of Samuel Barber's "Adagio for Strings." On both occasions, the sense of transcendence, of glory, coupled with a happiness that could not be put into words, was unforgettable. This may say nothing more than that I am unusually susceptible to cathartic emotional experiences when surrounded by loud music. But it might also serve to illustrate the wider point I am making. For every Pascal,

---

36 See the numerous examples provided in Martyn Lloyd-Jones, *Joy Unspeakable: The Baptism and Gifts of the Holy Spirit* (Eastbourne: Kingsway, 1995).

37 Augustine, *Confessions*, book VIII.

38 Augustine, *City of God*, book XX, chapter 8.

rendered speechless by an experience of the Spirit at bedtime, there is an Aquinas who has such a powerful revelation at Mass that he refuses to finish his magnum opus, the *Summa Theologica*. Being Eucharismatic makes people joyful, and it is the kind of joy that reaches the face.

🔥 🔥 🔥

Not everyone will be drawn to both. Historically, churches have usually centered corporate worship on one of three things—songs, sermons, or sacraments—and this presumably reflects the fact that different people, different church traditions, and different cultures will experience joy in God in different ways. We are shaped in this by our contexts, personalities, and histories. Our preferences are formed by leaders we have respected, examples we have admired, and excesses we have seen. Physical symbols will mean less in "low context" cultures (like most English speaking countries, where "hi" is a greeting and people wear T-shirts to church) than in "high context" cultures (where surroundings, gestures, clothes and greetings mean more than the words spoken). Most of us, for a whole host of reasons, will find some aspects of corporate worship easier to access, and to enjoy, than others.

But this actually strengthens the case for being both eucharistic and charismatic. If the church encompasses the whole body of Christ—cerebral and emotional, high and low context, introvert and extrovert, spontaneous and controlled, Asian, African, American, European, and so on—then local churches need to worship in ways that help *everyone* find joy in God, through Christ, by the Spirit. It is tempting for congregations to specialize, to cater exclusively for those who prefer songs, sermons, or sacraments. (Though contextualization is vital and in fact inevitable, it *can*, especially in Western cultures, become a euphemism for narrowing your focus and tailoring your brand for a specific target audience.) But the unintended consequence of this is the division of God's people: those who like quiet and routine go this way, those who like noise and spontaneity go that way, and the teenagers are in the room out back with the smoke machine.[39] Specialization in worship may help gather a crowd in the short term, but in the long term it kills diversity.

To be Eucharismatic, then, is to seek the joy of the whole church, even though most of us will find some components of corporate worship more appealing than others. For some, it will mean a call to praise him on the loud symbols, as well as the loud cymbals. For others, it will mean insisting on being happy-clappy rather than humpy-grumpy.[40] In many contexts, it will mean being quiet on some occasions and raucous on others. Yet for all of us, however we prefer to express it, it will mean pointing people to Jesus, crucified and risen, as the fountain of living waters, the end of our exploring, and the only source of everlasting joy.

---

39 This phenomenon of division by specialization is obvious in a "youth church," but is just as real in a church that only expresses worship in ways that noisy people or white people or reserved people find comfortable.
40 I owe this wonderful line to the inimitable Don Smith.

CHAPTER 4

EUCHARISTIC

What Do You Have That You Did Not Receive?

A rchitecture tells you a lot about what people value. A century ago, when the street I live on was being built, architects were carefully separating kitchens from dining rooms with walls and doors, so that domestic work could happen in an environment designed for it, without being seen or obstructed by guests or children or even men, and the spaces where people were received ("reception rooms") could be as pleasant and uncluttered as possible. For the last two decades, builders on the same street have been knocking those walls down to create larger kitchens, so that all of life can happen in one place: children's play, food preparation, the welcoming of guests, the serving of meals, audio-visual entertainment, maybe even paid work. The floor plans in my street reflect changes in society as a whole. We separate work and play, domestic and social, men and women, less than we used to; we also regard family meals, in which everyone sits down together without any distractions, as less important than our grandparents did. We can celebrate those developments or we can lament them, but they are there for all to see in the way we design our buildings. Architecture reveals priorities.

So it is with church buildings. Show me your architecture, and I'll show you your theology. Admittedly, some of the differences between church buildings across the centuries are merely a matter of technology (the availability or not of electric lighting, projector screens, amplification, heating, and so on). But most of them reflect—and then reinforce—theological priorities. High vaulted ceilings communicate grandeur. Stained glass windows with gospel scenes assume the legitimacy and importance of teaching through visual images. Crypts and graveyards communicate something about the memory of the faithful departed. Chancels, steps, and screens indicate a separation between the people and the priesthood. Bells, pews, soft chairs, kneelers, towers, coffee lounges, lecterns, video screens, spires, vestries, breast-feeding rooms, lighting rigs, organs—all of these embody assumptions about what the church is and how it functions. If a church has a cross-shaped layout or has the children's ministry in a separate wing or sits on top of a hill or faces east, it speaks to us. The very stones cry out.

Most striking of all is whatever is central. In all worship spaces, there is one central spot that our eyes are naturally drawn to as we enter the building. In an Orthodox church building, this might be the icon of Christos Pantokrator. In a Roman Catholic one, it would probably be the altar, where the Mass is celebrated. (In yet another sign of how layout communicates theology, the Protestant Reformers turned the "altar," which implies we are offering a sacrifice to God, into a "table," which makes it clear that God is offering a meal to us. Tweaking the furniture can have profound significance.) In many Presbyterian and Baptist sanctuaries it is the pulpit, where the Word of God is preached. In contemporary evangelical buildings, whether they are purpose-built warehouses, chapels, school halls, or theatres, our eye is usually drawn to the stage, on which you can see a band of musicians and, behind them, a screen. The centerpiece of a church's architecture usually reflects the centerpiece of its worship: singing, Communion, the preaching of the gospel, or whatever it may be.[1]

---

1 In some church traditions, including my own, corporate worship has been so colonized by singing that people use the word "worship" as if it actually *means* singing ("now so-and-so is going to preach from the Bible, and then after that we're going to have a time of worship").

Clearly, it is not as if an architectural emphasis on one feature has to diminish the significance of others, and it is perfectly possible to design a building in which a fusion of sermon, song, and sacrament converges on the center. Many Anglican churches, for instance, center on the Table flanked by the Word—with the lectern on one side and the pulpit on the other—with the choir facing each other immediately behind them. Other churches use the central space for a number of different purposes in the course of the service. Even so, it is probably fair to say that the focal point of a church's building and the focal point of its worship are closely connected—and, by the same token, if something is marginal spatially, it will probably be marginal in worship as well. Out of sight, out of mind.

Thus you can tell a lot about a church's theology and practice by simply standing in their building with your eyes open. In many worship spaces, for instance, one of the first architectural features you encounter on your way in is a baptismal font. You cannot find your seat without walking past it. So every time you come to worship with God's people, you face a small but insistent physical reminder that you have been baptized (or, of course, that you have not been baptized).[2] As soon as you have walked past it, you head down the nave—the chairs, or pews, are on either side—toward the large table that will later be used to celebrate the Lord's Supper. So in the very mundane act of entering the building and finding a seat, you walk unthinkingly between font and table, baptism and Communion. The message from the architecture is clear: sacraments are central to the Christian life around here.

Now consider a different experience. You enter the church building and see no physical features whatsoever that would suggest the sacraments exist. There is no font, no baptism pool, no altar, and no table.[3] If and when baptism happens, it happens in a nearby swimming pool. If and when the Eucharist happens, collapsible tables appear at the back, or in the aisles. In such a context, the message

---

2 Tish Harrison Warren, *Liturgy of the Ordinary* (Downers Grove: IVP, 2016), 17–18.

3 I hope it is obvious that this is not a criticism of churches (like the one I serve) whose baptism pools are under the floor and covered up to stop people falling in. Celebrating sacraments does not mean celebrating silliness.

from the architecture is equally clear: sacraments are occasional intrusions into our normal patterns of worship. They are like a mist that appears for a little time and then vanishes.

My point is not to recommend reshuffling our worship spaces, although in many cases that might not be a bad thing. Many New Testament churches met in homes and baptized people in rivers, and Jesus is present in the breaking of bread whether the table we use is made of oak, plastic, or nothing at all. My point is that the layout of our buildings reflects, and over time reinforces, our approach to the sacraments. So a church that has a permanent video screen, yet only has collapsible Communion tables, is also likely to be one in which videos are shown more often than the Lord's Supper is celebrated—and there is plenty of (admittedly anecdotal) evidence to suggest that this is actually the case. What we find space for, we will usually find time for. And lots of us, including most charismatics and many of those in garden variety evangelical churches, have less space and less time for the sacraments than Christians have typically had for twenty centuries.

In other words: we are not as eucharistic as we could be.

To anyone familiar with contemporary evangelicalism, that much is probably not news. Across the world, there are thousands upon thousands of churches, most of which are evangelical and many of which are also charismatic, in which neither baptism nor the Lord's Supper are celebrated on the average Sunday (and in which, on those Sundays when they are, they take up no more than a small fraction of the meeting time).[4] The conviction behind this chapter, however, is not merely that we *could* be more eucharistic than we are; it is that we *should* be more eucharistic than we are. The sacraments should be at the heart of our corporate worship, not peripheral and occasional interruptions to it. There is an "ought" here, not just an "is." That requires an explanation.

---

4 My very unscientific Twitter poll of just under 1,000 people revealed that 39% do not share the Lord's Supper on a typical week, and a further 33% allocate it less than a tenth of their meeting.

The explanation begins with Jesus. On the night he was "handed over"—by God, by the disciples, by Judas, by the soldiers, by the Sanhedrin, by Pilate, by Herod, by Pilate again, and in a sense by the entire human race—he took bread, and when he had given thanks, he broke it and said to them: "This is my body, which is for you. Do this in remembrance of me."[5] After supper he took the cup, saying: "This cup is the new covenant in my blood. Do this, as often as you drink it, in remembrance of me." As he inaugurated this mysterious meal, he connected it simultaneously to past, present, and future: back to the exodus ("I have earnestly desired to eat this Passover with you before I suffer"), forward to the new creation ("I will not drink again of this fruit of the vine until that day when I drink it new with you in my Father's kingdom"), and, of course, to the meaning of his own death in a few hours' time ("this is my blood of the covenant, which is poured out for many for the forgiveness of sins").[6] He also, in what would turn out to be probably the most controversial thing he ever said, identified the bread and wine as somehow *being* his body and blood.[7] In giving it both this meaning ("this is my . . .") and this regularity ("do this as often as you . . ."), Jesus ensured it would stand forever at the center of the church's worship as a tangible sign of his presence with his people, a means of participation ("communion") with him, and a reenactment of redemption, a physical symbol of our deliverance from slavery through his death and resurrection.[8]

Baptism, likewise, is a physical sign that represents our participation and union with Christ. Like the Eucharist, it reenacts our redemption from slavery to sin and death through the narrative and drama of the exodus from Egypt, as we, like Israel, go down into the waters and come out renewed, united, washed, and rescued from our enemies. Like the Eucharist, it is specifically connected in

---

5 1 Corinthians 11:23–25; the word *paradidōmi* can be translated "betray" or "hand over."

6 Matthew 26:26–29; Mark 14:22–25; Luke 22:14–23.

7 Christians have been burned, wars fought, and entire continents divided over that "somehow." My own view is expressed most succinctly in the Heidelberg Catechism, Q78–79.

8 For a superb reflection on the past, present, and future dimensions of the Lord's Supper, see Todd Billings, *Remembrance, Communion, and Hope: Rediscovering the Gospel at the Lord's Table* (Grand Rapids: Eerdmans, 2018).

the Gospels with the forgiveness of sins.[9] Like the Eucharist, it is a practice Jesus specifically commanded for all of his disciples: "Go therefore and make disciples of all nations, baptizing them in the name of the Father and of the Son and of the Holy Spirit."[10] Like the Eucharist, it was not only given to us but also modeled for us by Jesus who submitted to baptism not because he had sinned, but because it was necessary "to fulfill all righteousness."[11] The obvious difference between the two signs is that whereas the Lord's Supper is to be celebrated frequently, baptism only happens once. Yet their many similarities—external signs, instituted by Jesus in word and action, that convey forgiveness of sins, union with Christ, the presence of God, and the church's "exodus" through his death and resurrection—show why they have so often been marked off as distinct from other Christian practices, whether we call them "sacraments," "mysteries," "ordinances," or whatever.[12] Jesus said it; Jesus did it; that settles it.

The early church got the message. From the first day of the church, quite literally, the apostles insisted that Christianity required baptism—not just as a demonstration that a person had become a disciple, let alone as the sort of thing that Christians really ought to get around to at some point, but as part of the process of Christian initiation.[13] They went on to argue that baptism was how we put on Christ, are buried with Christ, raised with Christ, washed, and saved.[14] Modern evangelicals, nervous that these texts might imply salvation by works, hurry to explain that none of this means baptism actually *does* anything; it is just a symbol of what God has done

9 Mark 1:4; Luke 3:3.

10 Matthew 28:19.

11 Matthew 3:15.

12 Martin Luther famously concluded *The Babylonian Captivity of the Church* by arguing that there were not seven sacraments as in medieval Catholicism (Baptism, Communion, Penance, Confirmation, Holy Orders, Marriage, and Extreme Unction), but strictly speaking only two: "It has seemed best, however, to consider as sacraments, properly so called, those promises which have signs annexed to them. The rest, as they are not attached to signs, are simple promises. It follows that, if we speak with perfect accuracy, there are only two sacraments in the Church of God, Baptism and the Bread; since it is in these alone that we see *both a sign divinely instituted and a promise of remission of sins*" (emphasis added).

13 Acts 2:38; cf. 2:41; 8:12–13, 36–38; 9:18; 10:47–48; 16:15, 33; 18:8; 19:5; 22:16.

14 Romans 6:1–4; 1 Corinthians 6:11; Galatians 3:27; Colossians 2:11–12; 1 Peter 3:21–22.

inwardly. The apostles, on the other hand, were not so squeamish. As Paul puts it in Galatians: you are children of God through faith, for you have put on Christ in baptism.[15] The latter does not contradict the former, but rather provides the very reason for it.

At the same time, from the first day of the church, the disciples "devoted themselves . . . to the breaking of bread."[16] We know that this devotion continued, because decades later Luke describes a miracle as happening "on the first day of the week, when we were gathered together to break bread."[17] (As an aside, that is a fascinating and revealing summary of a Christian Sunday meeting. How many evangelical churches today could describe their services as "gathering together to break bread"?) When Paul brings teaching on the Lord's Supper, he matter-of-factly uses the phrase "when you come together" three times, as if one naturally involves the other.[18]

Furthermore, for Paul, Communion is not just a memorial or a symbol; it acts, bringing the church together with Christ and with one another. We are one, he explains, because we all share in one bread. We share a loaf of unity and a cup of blessing. As we do so, we proclaim the Lord's death until he comes. We actually participate in the body and blood of Christ. Consequently, if we do so in an unworthy way, we eat and drink judgment on ourselves.[19] The logic of statements like this is that in the Lord's Supper, just as in baptism, Christ is *presented* to us, not just *represented* to us. When we celebrate the sacraments, we do things that do things.

As we move out of Scripture and into the history of the church, we find all kinds of discussions and disagreements taking place over the nature of the sacraments.[20] But there is virtually unanimous

---

15 Galatians 3:26–27.

16 Acts 2:42.

17 Acts 20:7.

18 1 Corinthians 11:17–20. This connection flows both ways: breaking bread involves coming together, just as coming together involves breaking bread. It is not surprising that the rejection of the former, for instance in "online churches," has largely been confined to traditions that have already rejected the latter.

19 1 Corinthians 10:14–22; 11:27–32.

20 An excellent recent introduction is found in Justin Holcomb and David Johnson (ed.), *Christian Theologies of the Sacraments: A Comparative Introduction* (New York: NYU Press, 2017).

agreement that baptism and Eucharist are enormously powerful and enormously important. Their power and importance are connected, of course; the more you think the sacraments do, the more you are likely to think they matter. So across the world, in all branches of the church—Orthodox, Catholic, Nestorian, Oriental Orthodox, and eventually Protestant—the Eucharist became central to Christian worship. Baptism featured in the Apostles' Creed. And both were practiced in ways that communicated the transformative power and mysterious grace at work in the ordinary gifts of bread, wine, water, and oil.

Consider, for instance, how you experienced baptism and first Eucharist if you lived in Jerusalem in the fourth century.[21] First, you were catechized at length throughout Lent, in preparation for your baptism on Easter Eve. When the time came, you went down into an outer chamber, faced West, stretched out your hand as Moses did at the Red Sea, and renounced Satan and all his works. You then turned to face East, toward the sunrise, and affirmed your belief in Father, Son, and Holy Spirit, and in one baptism of repentance. Having done this, you proceeded to the inner chamber. You took off all your clothes, symbolizing the removal of the old humanity and your identification with Christ's sufferings. You were anointed with exorcised oil, representing the casting out of any powers of darkness. You approached the baptism pool, made another confession of faith, and then went down into the water three times, aligning yourself not only with the Trinity, but also with the three days Jesus was buried. On coming out of the water, you were anointed with oil on the forehead, ears, nostrils, and chest, the *chrism* indicating that you were now a Christian, and the body parts representing the removal of shame, ears to hear, the fragrance of Christ, and the breastplate of righteousness. Finally, you were given new, white clothes and were led back toward the sanctuary to sing a hymn, before receiving your first Eucharist.

My point is not that all churches today should do all of these things. Naked baptism would be a stretch in many cultures, I

---

21 Cyril of Jerusalem, *Mystagogic Lectures* I–III.

imagine.[22] My point is that baptismal practices like this reflect—and reinforce—a very high view of what baptism is: death, life, victory, burial, washing, renewal, anointing, and so on. They give a sense of the transformative, world-changing power of what is happening. They also get new believers off to a great start, both by starting their discipleship with pretty thorough catechesis and by framing their conversion in a narrative of exodus, grace, newness, lordship, and the overthrow of the devil.[23]

The sacraments, in that sense, enact the gospel. They dramatize our union with Christ in ways that words alone cannot. Clearly this can be enormously helpful in discipling all kinds of people: those from high-context cultures, oral learners, nonliterate communities, and so forth. Even in the most bookish societies it makes a huge difference when the Word is not just heard but also seen, felt, smelled, and tasted.

Not only that, but because they are so bound up with the presence of Jesus and the forgiveness of sins, the sacraments keep hoicking us back to the gospel, as long as they are accompanied by the preaching of the Word, so that the meaning of the symbols is plainly understood. John Wesley, one of the most effective evangelists of any generation, argued that it was the duty of Christians to receive Holy Communion as often as possible: "No man can have any pretense to Christian piety who does not receive it [not once a month, but] as often as he can."[24] Martin Luther, who emphasized the centrality of the gospel as

---

22 Although it is worth mentioning that this practice of baptism was single-sex, with female deacons baptizing female catechumens, and so on.

23 The argument of C. S. Lewis in *Mere Christianity* (New York: HarperCollins, 2001), 196–98, is relevant here. Lewis asks whether Christianity is hard or easy and replies that it is both: if you start off the easy way, then it is incredibly hard, but if you start off the hard way, it is incredibly easy. The more definitively you give up (and kill!) your old life as you start the Christian life, the easier your growth as a disciple becomes. On that basis, baptismal liturgies like this may have significant power in forming disciples. By starting out with such an emphatic renunciation of the old life, clothes, allegiances, and gods, the baptizand is given a huge advantage over those who experience a softer, more accommodating initiation. Easy come, easy go.

24 John Wesley, "The Duty of Constant Communion," in Albert Outler (ed.), *The Works of John Wesley* (Nashville: Abingdon, 1984), 3:427–39. Wesley's own summary of his argument is worth considering: "It has been shown, first, that if we consider the Lord's Supper as a command of Christ, no man can have any pretence to Christian piety, who does not receive it (not once a month, but) as often as he can. Secondly, that if we consider the institution of it, as a mercy to ourselves, no man who does not receive it as often as he can has any pretence to Christian

clearly as anyone, went so far as to say: "Now the mass is a part of the gospel; nay, the very sum and compendium of the gospel. . . . Hence also *sermons to the people ought to be nothing else but expositions of the mass*." [25]

The symbols explain the Word, and the Word explains the symbols. Put differently: If you want to be gospel-centered, be Table-centered. If you want to be truly evangelical, be eucharistic.

It is worth pausing for a moment to consider why, in so many church circles (including my own), it does not always seem this way. Why, given how central to Christian experience baptism and the Lord's Supper have always been—from Jesus, through the apostles, to pretty much the entire worldwide church until quite recently—are there so many churches today that would find the last few pages challenging or even bizarre? How have we ended up with entire denominations in which, on the basis of the space and time they allocate, the sacraments are relegated not just below preaching and singing but also below taking up the offering and even giving the notices? What is behind all this?

Several factors are at work, I think. For some, it is a visceral dislike of anything that seems routine or repetitive as opposed to spontaneous and free. For others, it is the association of symbols and rituals with formalism, "religion," and legalism. For others, the problem with particularly the Lord's Supper is its exclusivity: those who are not believers are not welcome to participate, which makes it awkward for guests and visitors in attendance. For others, the context is the issue; breaking bread should happen in homes, not on Sundays. Many of us grew up in churches where Communion was extremely boring, a lengthy and solemn section of the service in which the children did not seem welcome and the adults did not seem happy. Some

---

prudence. Thirdly, that none of the objections usually made, can be any excuse for that man who does not, at every opportunity obey this command and accept this mercy."

25 Luther, *Babylonian Captivity of the Church* (emphasis added).

(especially in larger churches) worry that it takes too long. Some find the whole process of taking Communion, especially the call to self-examination, to be introspective and uncomfortable. Many have simply been born or converted into churches that have never known anything different. There are probably other reasons as well.[26]

That requires some disentangling, at least if we want to do anything about it. It may be helpful to think about these various objections as forming a sort of spectrum. At the positive end, there is the insistence that the Lord's Supper should not be glum, incomprehensible, and tedious. Similarly, we should recognize that some ways of sharing Communion put such an emphasis on self-examination that all joy flies out the window; dancing turns into mourning, nobody would dream of calling it a "love feast," and if any observers were told it was a foretaste of a future meal, they would assume it was a funeral wake rather than a wedding banquet.[27]

Moving along the spectrum, we find objections that have some merit but need to be challenged nonetheless. Yes, the early church broke bread in their homes, but as we have seen, they also did it when they came together. Yes, the Lord's Supper can take a long time if there are hundreds or even thousands of people present, but then again there are many ways of celebrating it, and if the Jerusalem church managed it with five thousand members, then we probably can too.

But there are also reasons that need to be flatly rejected and, if necessary, publicly debunked. The sacraments are clearly religious—which, if James 1:27 is to be believed, is not a bad thing anyway—but in their embodiment of the gospel of grace they are the exact *opposite* of legalism (unless we are to accuse Jesus, the apostles, and most churches in history of legalism, which seems a little harsh). Routines and repetitive patterns in our worship (we could even call them "habits") are inevitable and, as we will see below, powerful. The "we've

---

26 Wesley, "The Duty of Constant Communion," cites and responds to five objections to regular Communion: (1) we feel unworthy, (2) we do not have enough time, (3) we diminish our reverence for it through habit, (4) we do not feel like we benefit from it, and (5) our church does not receive it regularly. *Plus ça change.*

27 The phrase *love feast* comes from Jude 12.

never done it like that" defense is, in a weird irony, the archetypal appeal to tradition, which is just what nonsacramental evangelicals are apparently trying to avoid. Furthermore, the separation that takes place when people go into the baptism pool, or approach the Lord's Table, is one of the most evangelistic moments in Christian worship, an explicit statement that people need to turn to Christ and be saved. Those who do not follow Jesus, and those who profess to but are currently in unrepentant sin, are welcome to sing, pray, read, give, and listen, and as a result could easily conclude that they need make no further response. To anyone in that position, simply by excluding some and including others, the sacraments proclaim, loud and clear: Repent of your sins, believe the gospel, and come to Christ.

Two further benefits of holding a high view of the sacraments, both pastoral in nature, are worth mentioning. The first is that the sacraments are a wonderful antidote to the fuzzy, shallow Gnosticism that characterizes Western culture today, in which the soul is the authentic self, the body is a malleable and fungible commodity that can be reconfigured through technology, and all things are subordinate to the will (usually expressed in terms of "choice"). Bodies are destroyed in utero, incinerated in death, redesigned in appearance, and reassigned in gender; the soul, and primarily the will to choose, is sacrosanct. Swimming in cultural waters like that can gnosticize the church, and a quick glance at the ecclesial landscape suggests that it has. A mixture of consumer preferences and accessible technology enables us to prioritize soul over body, experience over action, romance over love, choice over commitment, virtual over physical, anywhere over somewhere. *Vorsprung durch Technik*, as Audi puts it: "Progress through Technology."

Celebrating the sacraments draws us into a different and better story. It is thousands of years old, not shiny brand-new. It is repetitive, not innovative. It is unashamedly physical—hydrogen and oxygen, wheat and grapes, flesh and blood—and so takes us back to creation, in which God says that matter is good, and to the incarnation, in which God actually became flesh for us. It roots us in a particular place, with particular people. You can watch sermons online or sing worship songs in your car, but for the sacraments you actually have to *be* there, touching and smelling the elements in front of you and the people around you, and acknowledging the goodness of physical stuff as you participate.[28] As such, it is tricky to be eucharistic and gnostic at the same time.

The second benefit also relates to discipleship. Frequently, I come across the question: How can we welcome everybody into the church, no matter what their lifestyle, while making clear that certain types of behavior are incompatible with following Jesus? If a person has been coming to our church for years, and hearing the gospel preached regularly, but still shows no sign of repenting of X, Y, or Z, then how should pastors (and church members) respond? What does it look like, in this context, to exercise church discipline in a way that is full of grace and truth?

I think a large part of the answer is: Take the sacraments seriously. Dial them up, not down. Before you baptize people, teach them what Christians believe, how we live, how we pray. (There's a reason so many catechisms are structured around the Creed, the Ten Commandments, and the Lord's Prayer.) Be clear on repentance as well as faith. Make the process of dying and rising, renouncing old loyalties and embracing new ones, as explicit as possible in the way you baptize. Celebrate the Lord's Supper regularly, and make clear on what basis people are welcome to the Table. If a person refuses to repent of X, Y, or Z, explain to them why they should not participate until they have. Such an approach avoids ignoring sin but also avoids a perfectionist exclusivity that only allows people to come to church if their lives are already sorted out. It's a version of the point Jesus made in the parable of the wedding banquet: everyone is invited to the wedding, but those who share in the feast need to be wearing appropriate clothes.[29] It is also, as far as we can tell, how Paul instructed the church in Corinth. Unbelievers and enquirers are welcome to join in your meetings—but the Lord's Supper is for those who worship God, forsake sin, and share in Christ.[30]

---

28 There is probably a connection between the Roman Catholic Church's emphasis on the sacraments, their robust theology of the body, and their (so far) fairly unwavering response to the sexual revolution. I owe this point to Professor Carl Trueman.

29 Matthew 22:1–14.

30 Compare, e.g., 1 Corinthians 14:23–25 (on unbelievers in worship) with 5:11; 10:14, 18–22; 11:27–32 (on the need for godliness, worship of God alone, and self-examination).

The sacraments, then, are biblically commanded, historically warranted, cross-culturally wise, evangelistically significant, and pastorally helpful. More than that, though, they are God-given ways of sharing in Christ, experiencing the work of the Spirit, drawing close to the Father, and enacting the gospel. As such, celebrating them regularly, and making much of them when we do, is not just dutiful or useful but beautiful.[31] It may mean departing from our tradition or rearranging the schedule (or even the furniture), but it will be worth it.

That, believe it or not, was the easy bit. No matter how "low church" we are, we all know that baptism and Communion are good things and that Jesus gave them to us and that our churches would ultimately be deficient without them. At the start of this book, however, I described "eucharistic" churches not just as unashamedly sacramental, but as historically rooted, deliberately liturgical, and self-consciously catholic. That may be a tougher sell.

Perhaps not when it comes to history. Human beings love stories, and we want to know where we come from, so we naturally give an account of how our church, network, or denomination came to be. Those Protestants who emphasize continuity—Lutherans, Anglicans, the Reformed, some varieties of Baptists and Methodists, and so on—inevitably highlight historical roots as we do so, tracing them back to the Reformation (and often beyond it, through medieval Catholicism right back to the church fathers). Those of us who stress discontinuity, and portray the institutional church as the dark backdrop against which the bright light of our movement first began to shine, may prefer to find our heritage in protest movements and martyrs (Montanists, Donatists, Cathars, Waldensians, Lollards, Hussites, Anabaptists, Huguenots, Puritans, Moravians, Nonconformists, and

---

31 I have deliberately avoided spelling out what *regularly* might mean; personally my preference is weekly, but there is no text of Scripture that requires it. My point here, in the end, is about more than just frequency. It is possible to celebrate Communion weekly in a way that trivializes or minimizes it, just as it is possible to celebrate it monthly in a way that makes much of it.

the rest), or even in monasticism. Chances are, though, that all of us will lay claim to historical roots of some sort.

Not all of those roots will be self-consciously catholic, however. I doubt I am the only evangelical pastor who, on leading my church to recite the Nicene Creed, has had puzzled members of the congregation approach me afterward to ask why on earth we are saying "we believe in one holy, catholic and apostolic church." Some of that is just a matter of terminology: in modern English, the word *catholic* sounds like it means "Roman" as opposed to "universal," so people unfamiliar with the language will assume that the *catholic* church is the one with the pope.[32] But some of it may go deeper, reflecting a self-understanding that is more sectarian than universal. We are the true, the pure, the radical church, in contrast to the compromised, stuffy, carnal, unbiblical, and even idolatrous institution(s) over there. In my British charismatic context, that perspective is summed up beautifully by the following diagram of the church's history, which appeared in a magazine in the 1980s:[33]

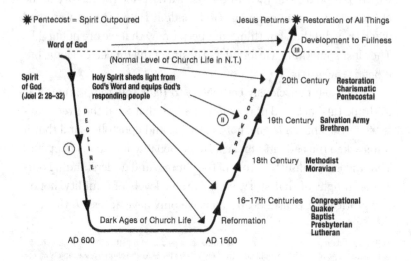

32 The Greek *katholikos* derives from the word *katholou* ("in general"), which itself is a combination of *kata* ("according to") and *holos* ("the whole").

33 *Restoration Magazine* (Nov/Dec 1983), 40.

Admittedly, this is a somewhat cartoonish example. Most of us would raise our eyebrows at any historical account that writes off the fathers, the creeds, the evangelization of the known world, and the emergence of Christian civilization as "decline," or the age of Christian hospitals, universities, philosophers, and cathedrals as the "dark ages." We would also be suspicious of its ethnocentrism—the chart would not look remotely like this if you were Syrian, Abyssinian, Russian, or Chinese, or if your ancestors were shipped in chains across the Middle Passage—and its disregard for the unity of the church.[34] More than that: we would worry about the arrogance of making our generation the high point of history, and the theological implications of what on earth God was doing for the first fifteen hundred years. Was the Light of the World snuffed out by the darkness of his people? Was the Spirit on an extended holiday?

Yet we may recognize the shape of the narrative, all the same. Stories move from problem to solution and incline us to see ourselves (or people like us) as part of the solution, so it is not surprising that we are tempted to do the same when we describe the history of the church. This went wrong, but God made it right. Things were bad when they did that, but things are better now that we are doing this. They lost something; we found it. The arc of the universe is long, but it bends toward us.

To be self-consciously catholic is to fight this temptation. It is to think, talk, act, and pray as if we believe that what the Creed says is true—the church is one, holy, catholic, and apostolic—and that if Jesus asked the Father to make us one, then it will actually happen.[35] That involves telling the story of the church, and understanding ourselves in light of that story, with suitable levels of humility, honor, and gratitude.[36] Gratitude, because we only have access to the doc-

---

34 If the X-axis represented the number of ethnic groups united together into one church, the U-bend shape of the chart would be turned entirely on its head: the church grew rapidly across the world in the first few hundred years while remaining united, then stabilized as a result of limitations in travel and the growth of Islam, and then fragmented into first dozens, then hundreds, then thousands of denominations following the Protestant Reformation.

35 John 17:20–23.

36 This does not mean flattening the story to ensure that all generations are presented as equally

trine of the Trinity, the gospel, the Bible, and so on through the efforts and sacrifices of those who have gone before us: saints and scholars, popes and patriarchs, monks, mystics, and martyrs. Honor, because many of them made massive sacrifices in the process, and almost all of them lived their daily lives in conditions that were immeasurably less pleasant than ours. Humility, because for all of our differences with many of them, they got an awful lot right, we get an awful lot wrong, and the same Holy Spirit who works in us was at work in them.[37] Frankly, I cannot imagine anyone reading Augustine, Gregory Nazianzen, Thomas Aquinas, John Calvin, or Blaise Pascal and *not* being deeply humbled by how small we are, whether we were aiming to or not. Being eucharistic in this broader, catholic sense entails thankfulness—*eucharistia*—for the church across time and across the world. And it expresses itself in appreciation, respect, and prayer in and through our disagreements.

For many of us, I imagine, the most alien aspect of this book is the invitation to be deliberately liturgical. To us, the very word *liturgy* smells of death. It evokes arcane language, disengaged chanting, and dust clouds billowing out of the organ loft. Our version of Christianity is about freedom and spontaneity, not empty repetition. We let the Spirit blow where he will, making each meeting different, rather than following the same form of words, every week. We swapped liturgy for liberty a long time ago and have no plans to go back.

To which one obvious response is: no, we didn't. We didn't get rid of our liturgy; we changed it. In some cases, we made a direct swap—a

---

positive. Few historians would deny that the fourth century was a high point in the church's story or that the fourteenth century was unusually difficult. It does, however, mean owning both the successes and the failures, since we are all one body, and doing our best to understand (and learn from) both.

37 "Tradition means giving votes to the most obscure of all classes, our ancestors. It is the democracy of the dead. Tradition refuses to submit to the small and arrogant oligarchy of those who merely happen to be walking about. All democrats object to men being disqualified by the accident of birth; tradition objects to their being disqualified by the accident of death" (Chesterton, *Orthodoxy*, 205).

welcome instead of a call to worship, an offering instead of a collection, a midmeeting interval to greet one another instead of "the peace," a closing prayer instead of a benediction. In other cases, we got rid of some things that get said every week (the Creed, the Lord's Prayer, the comfortable words), and replaced them with some other things that get said every week (like "the Lord inhabits the praises of his people" or "let's sing a new song to the Lord" or "if you're visiting, we're not after your money" or "please stick around for coffee after the meeting"). Most obviously, we continue to chant set phrases of prayer and worship that were written by somebody else, often several times in the same service (as long as they are set to music). If I know that somebody attends a contemporary evangelical or charismatic church, I can make a pretty good guess as to what their order of worship will be, even if I have never been there.[38] The reports of liturgy's death are greatly exaggerated.

We can say much more than that, though. Yes, a set order of worship is more or less inevitable, and therefore it makes sense to ensure that ours is as spiritual and biblical as possible.[39] But even this statement could make repeated worship practices sound like an unavoidable pitfall, a necessary nuisance that we might as well learn to live with. We need to go beyond that. Liturgy is not merely neutral, but positive. It is not just inevitable, but powerful. It can train us, shape our habits, and reorient our desires. So it is helpful for us to see how formative liturgy is and, more than that, how graceful—how full of *charis*—it can be.

The best recent argument for the formative power of liturgy, at least that I have come across, is found in James K. A. Smith's book *Desiring the Kingdom*.[40] (The only downside of this is that it is also one of the

---

38 This point is often made through satire, as in North Point Media's "Contemporvant" video, or The Babylon Bee's article, "Local Church Sings '10,000 Reasons' for 10,000th Time."

39 I remember asking a friend at university why his church used the Book of Common Prayer. His reply had never even occurred to me: "The basic idea is that we all get into habits in our worship, so they might as well be good ones."

40 James K. A. Smith, *Desiring the Kingdom: Worship, Worldview, and Cultural Formation* (Grand

most frequently summarized recent arguments for anything, so if you have already read the book, or an overview of it, you may want to skip this next section.)[41] Evangelicals today, Smith explains, tend to assume that the way to make disciples and form character is to give people information, whether in education or in church. We teach and instruct people, in pulpits, classrooms, and lecture halls, and trust that the knowledge they have will change their worldview, which will lead them to make good choices and become more like Jesus. When they do something silly, we ask incredulously, "What were you *thinking*?" We treat people, that is, as if they are fundamentally *knowers*.

Only we aren't. Fundamentally, as Augustine saw, we are *lovers*. The most defining feature of our character is not what we know, but what we love, whether we can fully articulate it or not. So to truly form a person, you have to get to their hearts, their desires, their affections.

These loves are not formed logically. We may not even know what they are, let alone where they came from. Smith presents a fascinating challenge from Andrei Tarkovsky's movie *Stalker*: if you could walk into a room in which your deepest desire would become a reality—but with the proviso that it would be what your deepest desire *really* is, rather than what you *think* it is—would you go in? Or would you hesitate, fearful that, like Kevin Spacey in *American Beauty*, getting what we want might not be all it was cracked up to be?[42] Sometimes, Smith argues, we do not love what we think. Loves are not rationally deduced, or even cognitive. We learn to love and to desire long before we learn to think logically.

Further, our loves are shaped in large part by our habits. They involve our bodies and our emotions, not just our minds. Developing them is more like learning to drive or playing the piano or practicing

---

Rapids: Baker, 2009).

41 Smith's argument has sparked a whole host of insightful writings from younger evangelicals, all of whom summarize his case, on topics ranging from sex (Jonathan Grant, *Divine Sex: A Compelling Vision for Christian Relationships in a Hypersexualized Age* [Grand Rapids: Brazos, 2015]), to ambition (Jen Pollock Michel, *Teach Us to Want: Longing, Ambition and the Life of Faith* [Downers Grove: IVP, 2014]), to daily life (Warren, *Liturgy of the Ordinary*), not to mention Smith's summary of his own work in *You Are What You Love* (Grand Rapids: Brazos, 2016).

42 Smith, *You Are What You Love*, 27–32.

a golf swing, than it is like learning algebra or history. They are shaped by our routines, our rituals, our practices, and particularly those "thick" practices—or, we could say, liturgies—that form our identities and aim at a particular vision of the good life.

The modern world sees this more clearly than the modern church. In a famous passage, Smith walks us through the secular liturgy of shopping at a mall: we enter the sanctuary, have our eyes drawn skyward to the vaulted ceiling, pass through the central meeting area, wander through various side chapels (shops) browsing their different offerings, experience multisensory worship through music, lighting, food, drink, aromas and the like, see icons (mannequins and posters) pointing to an idealized version of the good life, make transactions at altars (tills) in order to get closer to it, and receive a benediction (have a nice day). Later he does something similar with the way in which military pride is cultivated in American sporting events and shows how the practices (standing, singing the national anthem, spreading a flag across the field, military flyovers whose sound reverberates in the chest, cheering across the stadium) shape the desires of the people there far more than any information could.

The reason for all this is that marketers—and American patriots— have a fuller, more holistic view of the human person than many Christians do. They recognize the importance of patterns of behavior that form the heart, not just information that shapes the mind. "We are," Smith writes, "ultimately *liturgical animals* because we are fundamentally desiring creatures. . . . We are embodied, practicing creatures whose love/desire is aimed at something ultimate."[43] If you want to shape people's lives, you don't just need to shape their logic; you need to shape their loves, which probably also means shaping their liturgies.

If Smith is right—and despite some minor objections I think he basically is—then three things follow for Christian discipleship.[44]

---

43 Smith, *Desiring the Kingdom*, 40.

44 I see three main challenges to Smith's broad argument, although there are probably others. (1) It is very possible to be a fundamentally secular consumer in our choice of traditional piety; low church evangelicals have not cornered the market on liturgical brand preferences or ecclesial shopping. "Even the return to traditional liturgy that one finds in some circles can be driven by the same underlying forces of expressive individualism. Rather than a submission to authority,

The first is that our liturgy is the most powerful corporate disciple-making tool we have available. This may seem outlandish. Disciples are made in many ways: in families, through personal times of prayer and reading Scripture, in small groups, in one-to-one relationships, through suffering, and so on, as well as in church gatherings. Yet when we consider the means of Christian formation we have at our disposal *corporately*—the things we are able to do together, as opposed to the things we can encourage people to do in their daily lives—then nothing has more power than our liturgy: the things we say, hear, and do when we meet for worship. If we want to be trained to pray, nothing is more effective than corporate prayer. If we want to be trained to turn from sin, nothing is more effective than corporate confession. If we want to be trained in the Bible, nothing is more effective than hearing it read and declaring it out loud, with or without music. Reading it is good; hearing it is better; speaking and hearing it, best of all. Ask any child. So it always surprises me when I hear of churches who allocate three quarters of their Sunday service to a sermon on the basis that it is the best way of

---

tradition can be an attractive consumer choice for those in search of 'authenticity' in a society where many options on offer seem to lack the weight and beauty of long-established custom. Attending a church with a higher liturgy can be a worshiper's means of signaling refinement, elevated aesthetic judgment, ecclesiastical pedigree, and socio-economic class. In such cases, tradition may be valued principally for its vintage feel or ancient dignity, rather than for the truth that first animated its creation" (Alastair Roberts, "Liturgical Piety," in *Our Secular Age: Ten Years of Reading and Applying Charles Taylor*, ed. Collin Hansen [Deerfield: TGC, 2017], 63–73, at 69). (2) Practically, if the shape and content of our liturgy is as powerful as Smith suggests, then the Church of England, complete with the Book of Common Prayer, ought to be making more and better disciples than Pentecostal house churches in China, which it clearly isn't. In his recent work, Smith wrestles with a similar objection (which he calls "The *Godfather* problem," after the climax of Francis Ford Coppola's film) at some length; see James K. A. Smith, *Awaiting the King: Reforming Public Theology* (Grand Rapids: Brazos, 2017), 165–208. On the question of the relationship between liturgy and behavior, the study of Christian Scharen, *Public Worship and Public Work: Character and Commitment in Local Congregational Life* (Collegeville: Liturgical Press, 2004) is worth noting: worship is not so much formation as "con-formation, a reinforcement and reminder of what is important in life as they envision it in that place" (at 221). (3) Glenn Packiam argues that Smith stresses worship as formation (a Reformed emphasis) far more than as mission (an evangelical emphasis), and almost entirely neglects worship as encounter (a Pentecostals-charismatic emphasis). This may be missing something important, since the evidence suggests Pentecostal-charismatics are more engaged in (say) practical service to their neighbors than other branches of the church, as argued by Donald Miller and Tetsunao Yamamori, *Global Pentecostalism: The New Face of Christian Social Engagement* (Berkeley: University of California Press, 2007). The answer to these last two objections, in my view, is to be Eucharismatic—but then I would say that, wouldn't I?

grounding people in Scripture; this strikes me as somewhat naïve about how we come to learn things, let alone about how we come to love things. Despite appearances, I suspect the boot is usually on the other foot.

The power of our liturgy is enhanced by the fact that its impact continues beyond the Sunday service. The elements we include in our corporate gatherings will inevitably influence our view of what worship *is*, and therefore shape the things we do when we are together in small groups or prayer meetings or Bible studies or family devotions or even on our own. If our Sunday meetings are comprised entirely of singing and listening to sermons, then the chances are that we will grow to think of spirituality as primarily about those two things (and from there, it is a relatively small step to simply listening to Christian music and sermon downloads). By contrast, if they involve reading, hearing, praying, singing, confessing, declaring, giving, eating, and drinking, we are more likely to regard those practices as normal aspects of Christian discipleship, and to bring them into our daily lives. Unsurprisingly, our patterns of worship when we are scattered are shaped by our patterns of worship when we are gathered. Good liturgy is a gift that keeps on giving.

Our second takeaway regarding discipleship, which is closely related to this, is that we need to think carefully about the content of our liturgy. Were we all to undertake a thoughtful audit of the elements present in our church's worship, as compared to those in the New Testament, those of the church through history, and those of the global church today, it might well reveal that we have nothing to be concerned about. But it might reveal various practices that, though biblically and historically rooted, have been jettisoned for pragmatic or traditional reasons, and could be retrieved for the benefit of everybody. Here, for example, is a list of twenty such practices, along with biblical instances of each, and examples of ways in which they bring benefit to the church.[45] It is far from exhaustive, but it might provide a starting point for such an audit, and prompt reflection on what our ancestors prioritized, what we prioritize, and why:

---

45 This list is similar, but not identical, to the list given (with explanations of each) in Smith, *Desiring the Kingdom*, 155–214. Good examples of virtually all of these practices can be found in, among other places, *The Book of Common Prayer*.

PRACTICE	SCRIPTURAL EXAMPLE	BENEFITS TO THE CHURCH
1. Call to worship	"Come, let us sing for joy to the LORD! Let us shout aloud to the Rock of our salvation!" (Psalm 95:1 NIV)	Focuses us on God and his goodness at the beginning. Provides a clear starting point.
2. God's greeting to us	"Grace to you and peace from him who is and who was and who is to come, and from the seven spirits who are before his throne, and from Jesus Christ the faithful witness, the firstborn of the dead, and the ruler of kings on earth." (Revelation 1:4–5)	Reminds us that God is already present, and that he is welcoming us as much as we are welcoming him. Begins the service with God's work rather than ours.
3. Our greeting to one another	"Greet one another with a holy kiss. All the churches of Christ greet you." (Romans 16:16)	Physically enacts what it is to be a family. Welcomes guests. Includes everybody.
4. Baptism	"Go therefore and make disciples of all nations, baptizing them in the name of the Father and of the Son and of the Holy Spirit." (Matthew 28:19)	Enacts the defeat of sin, the washing away of sin, being drenched in the Spirit, burying the old life, and rising again to new life.
5. Singing	"Be filled with the Spirit, addressing one another in psalms and hymns and spiritual songs, singing and making melody to the Lord with your heart." (Ephesians 5:18–19)	Expresses and cultivates joy. Articulates lament, expectation, and hope. Teaches theology. Encourages creativity in music and dance. Develops thankfulness.
6. Prayer	"... praying at all times in the Spirit, with all prayer and supplication. To that end, keep alert with all perseverance, making supplication for all the saints, and also for me." (Ephesians 6:18–19)	Teaches us how to pray, by drawing on the prayers of others. Highlights that prayer is a corporate activity not just a solo one ("Our Father ..."). Reinforces solidarity with the worldwide church.
7. Reading the Old Testament	"Until I come, devote yourself to the public reading of Scripture." (1 Timothy 4:13)	Exposes sin. Points us to our need for Christ. Instructs us in Christian living.

PRACTICE	SCRIPTURAL EXAMPLE	BENEFITS TO THE CHURCH
8. Confession	"Confess your sins to one another and pray for one another, that you may be healed." (James 5:16)	Encourages us to renounce sin specifically and corporately, not vaguely and individually. Shows us our need for grace.
9. Assurance of forgiveness	"If you forgive the sins of any, they are forgiven them; if you withhold forgiveness from any, it is withheld." (John 20:23)	Heals our consciences. Assures us that God's grace is greater than our sin. Debunks the accusations of the devil.
10. Using spiritual gifts	"When you come together, each one has a hymn, a lesson, a revelation, a tongue, or an interpretation. Let all things be done for building up." (1 Corinthians 14:26)	Encourages us to function as an interdependent body, not a front-led show. Demonstrates to unbelievers that God is really among us. Builds us up.
11. The Creed	"For I delivered to you as of first importance what I also received: that Christ died for our sins in accordance with the Scriptures, that he was buried, that he was raised on the third day in accordance with the Scriptures, and that he appeared to Cephas, then to the twelve." (1 Corinthians 15:3–5)	Centers on the Trinity. Reinforces solidarity with the church across history and across the world. Keeps us focused on the primary truths of Christianity. Teaches theology, especially the doctrine of God. Provides a framework for catechesis.
12. Reading the Gospels	"It seemed good to me also, having followed all things closely for some time past, to write an orderly account for you, most excellent Theophilus, that you may have certainty concerning the things you have been taught." (Luke 1:3–4)	Centers the church on the life, death, and resurrection of Jesus. Builds faith. Grounds us in the gospel. Challenges us to live zealous Christian lives. Reinforces the supernatural shape of Christianity.
13. Reading the Epistles	"I put you under oath before the Lord to have this letter read to all the brothers." (1 Thessalonians 5:27)	Expounds the implications of the life, death, and resurrection of Jesus, and applies them to us. Equips us. Teaches and encourages us.

PRACTICE	SCRIPTURAL EXAMPLE	BENEFITS TO THE CHURCH
14. Preaching and teaching	"I charge you in the presence of God and of Christ Jesus, who is to judge the living and the dead, and by his appearing and his kingdom: preach the word; be ready in season and out of season; reprove, rebuke, and exhort, with complete patience and teaching." (2 Timothy 4:1–2)	Heralds the good news of what God has done for us in Christ, and how we should respond. Explains the meaning of God's Word, so that we can be shaped and changed by it. Exhorts and encourages us. Engages with unbelievers.
15. Eucharist	"For as often as you eat this bread and drink the cup, you proclaim the Lord's death until he comes." (1 Corinthians 11:26)	Unites us to Christ and to one another. Proclaims the Lord's death until he comes. Enacts thankfulness. Brings joy.
16. Offering	"On the first day of every week, each of you is to put something aside and store it up, as he may prosper, so that there will be no collecting when I come." (1 Corinthians 16:2)	Puts God first where it hurts most. Prioritizes the ordinary work of the local church. Serves the poor. Supports the ministry of the gospel.
17. Blessing	"The grace of the Lord Jesus Christ and the love of God and the fellowship of the Holy Spirit be with you all." (2 Corinthians 13:14)	Closes the meeting with grace, just as it opened. Concludes by reminding us of God's goodness and favor.
18. Commission as witnesses	"But you will receive power when the Holy Spirit has come upon you, and you will be my witnesses in Jerusalem and in all Judea and Samaria, and to the end of the earth." (Acts 1:8)	Esteems the ordinary work of Monday to Saturday. Connects the Lord's Day gathering with the rest of the Christian life. Reinforces the mission to which we are called.
19. The lectionary	"Therefore I testify to you this day that I am innocent of the blood of all, for I did not shrink from declaring to you the whole counsel of God." (Acts 20:26–27)	Ensures that a wide range of Scripture is covered in a year. Prevents a church's biblical diet from being too shaped by pastors' styles or preferences.

20. The church calendar	"For Paul had decided to sail past Ephesus, so that he might not have to spend time in Asia, for he was hastening to be at Jerusalem, if possible, on the day of Pentecost." (Acts 20:16)	Orients the shape of the whole year in the Christian story. Communicates the value of seasons and rhythms. Encourages both fasting and feasting. Narrates the gospel.

The third takeaway regarding discipleship is that we need to reflect not just on our liturgy's content, but on its shape. Corporate worship is not a series of unrelated practices thrown together without sequence; our liturgy tells a story, and the shape of this story forms our imagination at least as much as the practices do. (In Smith's neat phrase, restoring people involves restorying people.) If we are not attentive to the shape of the story, then we can easily end up in silliness at best, implicit legalism at worst. A service that began with confession, for instance, would put the accent on the way we approach God in the wrong place. More pointedly, a service that began with forty minutes of expressive praise, suffused with the language of pursuing God's presence and waiting for him to come, without a clear proclamation of how God has already come near to us in Christ, would communicate that encountering God is basically about our climbing the mountain rather than his descending it. Without meaning to, it would diminish the gracious initiative of God. It would lack grace or *charis*.

A well-structured liturgy, on the other hand, can reinforce the call-and-response dynamic of the gospel; it can be, literally, grace-full. God has welcomed us, so now we can welcome each other. God's Word exposes our sins, we confess them, and he forgives them. God speaks, and then we speak. Christ has offered himself for us, so now we bring our offerings to him. God acts, then we act. We breathe in revelation, then we breathe out response.[46] Grace, then gratitude. If structured

---

46 This excellent phrase has become one of the hallmarks of the contemporary worship leader Matt Redman.

carefully, with gospel-like elements in a gospel-like order, a liturgy can be evangelical in the best sense. In centering on the grace of God, and our response of thankfulness, it can also be genuinely *eucharistic*.[47]

All of which being said, the most compelling case for liturgical practice—as for eucharistic practice in general—will not be found in an argument or a book, but in actually doing it.[48] It is hard to explain to someone who has never tried bungee jumping or Beethoven why they should; the proof of the pudding is in the eating. No argument for creeds or hymns can rival the power of actually reciting the Nicene Creed or singing "When I Survey the Wondrous Cross" with your brothers and sisters.[49] No argument for Cranmer's wedding service

---

47 There is a horizontal as well as a vertical dimension to this. Vertically, good liturgy catches us up in thankfulness to God. But allowing our liturgy to be shaped by our ancestors also catches us up in horizontal gratitude: it involves the acknowledgment that we are receiving both the content and the shape of our liturgy as *gifts* from men and women who thought carefully about them, practiced them amidst circumstances that were far more challenging and physically painful than most of ours, and in some cases died for them (Thomas Cranmer, as so often, is the classic example). In his introduction to Athanasius' *On the Incarnation*, C. S. Lewis urges people to read old books, because the errors of our own generation are likely only to be challenged by those from previous centuries. If this is true of books, it is surely also true of prayers, hymns, creeds, liturgies, and catechisms—and continuing to use them expresses thankfulness to them, for helping to identify our blind spots and drawing us into truly catholic worship, as well as to God.

48 Having said which, there are obviously anecdotal arguments for the power of liturgy. As part of a training course for pastors a few years ago, I asked the group whether they thought a person needed to have turned away from all their sins before being baptized, or whether it was sufficient to have believed and confessed in Jesus. One person said no: in our church, we just ask people whether a person trusts in Jesus as their Lord and Savior. Another person said yes: in our church, we ask people if they have *repented of their sins* and put their trust in Jesus. Unwittingly, both were arguing *from* their liturgy *to* their theology and practice of baptism, not the other way around (and I doubt this situation is unique). Liturgy trains.

49 Ben Myers has a super passage at the start of his *The Apostles' Creed: A Guide to the Ancient Catechism* (Bellingham: Lexham Press, 2018) in which he traces the similarities between repeating creeds and repeating wedding vows, rather than making up our own: "Christians today are often suspicious of creeds. Many churches are more comfortable with mission statements than with creeds. The thing about a mission statement is you always get to make it up for yourself. It's like writing your own wedding vows. But here's the paradox. It is the individualised confession, like the personalised wedding vow, that ends up sounding like an echo of the wider society. . . . By contrast, to confess the creed is to take up a countercultural stance. When we say the creed we are not just expressing our own views or our own priorities. We are joining our voices to a great communal voice that calls out across the centuries from every tribe and tongue. We locate ourselves as part of that community that transcends time and place. That gives us a critical distance from our own time and place. If our voices are still echoes, they are now echoing something from beyond our own cultural moment."

could have the same power as hearing yet another young couple pledge "to have and to hold, from this day forward, for better, for worse, till death us do part," in imitation of the covenant promises made between Christ and the church. No argument for catechisms can compete with corporately asking and answering question 1 of the Heidelberg Catechism:

> Q. What is your only comfort in life and in death?
> A. That I am not my own, but belong—body and soul, in life and in death—to my faithful Saviour, Jesus Christ. He has fully paid for all my sins with his precious blood, and has set me free from the tyranny of the devil. He also watches over me in such a way that not a hair can fall from my head without the will of my Father in heaven; in fact, all things must work together for my salvation. Because I belong to him, Christ, by his Holy Spirit, assures me of eternal life and makes me wholeheartedly willing and ready from now on to live for him.

And no argument for set prayers can hold a candle to confessing your sins like this:

> Almighty God, our heavenly Father,
> we have sinned against you
> and against our neighbour
> in thought and word and deed,
> through negligence, through weakness,
> through our own deliberate fault.
> We are truly sorry
> and repent of all our sins.
> For the sake of your Son Jesus Christ,
> who died for us,
> forgive us all that is past
> and grant that we may serve you in newness of life
> to the glory of your name.
> Amen.

To which the pastor then responds:

> May Almighty God,
> who forgives all who truly repent,
> have mercy upon us,
> pardon and deliver us from all our sins,
> confirm and strengthen us in all goodness,
> and keep us in life eternal;
> through Jesus Christ our Lord. Amen.

Talk about amazing grace.

There is a certain humility to eucharistic Christianity. It forces us to acknowledge how small we are in the grand scheme of things, how reliant on the theological insights, evangelistic efforts, and faithful prayers of others. It challenges both our ethnocentrism and our chronological snobbery, as we declare truths and say prayers written by Asians, Africans, Europeans, and Americans who lived and died before anesthetics or electricity. It balances our self-assessment: yes, we are the most likely generation in history to be able to contextualize the gospel to twenty-first-century people, but we are also the most likely people in history to have swallowed the twenty-first-century *zeitgeist* without realizing it. It reminds us of the interdependence and interconnectedness of Christ's global and historic church. It encourages us to think of ourselves not as stand-alone saplings that have sprung up out of nowhere in the last few years, but as twigs in an enormous oak tree that are still fed and sustained by its giant roots. So, as Paul said in another context, if you now share in the nourishing roots of the tree, do not be arrogant toward the other branches.

More basically still, to be eucharistic is to be thankful. It means receiving all the sacramental, liturgical, and historical gifts that God has given to his church with glad and grateful hearts. It involves seeing our legacy as a gift, both in the strengths that sustain us (prayers, creeds, confessions, missions, songs, sacrifices, art, courage), and in the weaknesses that warn us (divisions, wars, moral failures, compromises, injustices, abuses of power, persecutions, and the rest).[50] And it urges us, even compels us, to consider the great cloud of witnesses—the communion of saints, dead and alive, with whom we share one Lord, one loaf, one cup, one baptism—and give thanks to him who has brought us into one holy, catholic, and apostolic church. For what do we have that we did not receive?

---

50 For a brief meditation on the latter, see my "The Strange Encouragement of the Church's Appalling History," *Christianity Today* (April 2017).

CHAPTER 5

CHARISMATIC
Zealously Desire Spiritual Gifts

There is a sense in which this book so far has begged the question. Some of you, especially those from more conservative backgrounds, may be exasperated that a biblical defense of charismatic practice has been deferred until now. It is quite intentional, however: Blaise Pascal persuaded me awhile ago that theological arguments do not take place on a blank canvas, and that before demonstrating that something is true, you have to first show that it is worthy of respect and then make people want it to be true. Only then can you expect to be heard when you argue that it is.[1]

Nevertheless, for most readers, vision casting and anecdotes will not be enough. What is needed now is an explanation of why charismatic practice—the pursuit of both the gifts and the experience of the Holy Spirit—is biblical. Here goes.

---

1 Blaise Pascal, *Pensées* (London: Penguin, 1995), 4.

🔥 🔥 🔥

The early church was a charismatic community. Of that there can be no doubt. From the day of Pentecost onward, the book of Acts is a story of Spirit baptism, speaking in other languages, prophesying, healing, casting out demons, angelic encounters, miraculous prison breaks, visions, dreams, evangelistic preaching, buildings shaking, the dead being supernaturally brought to life (and, on occasion, the living being supernaturally brought to death), boldness in the face of persecution, joy, and even teleportation. I have read a fair few accounts of miracles and revivals, some of them fairly extreme, but I have never seen any claims that compare to Acts in scope, frequency, or drama.

Acts is not an anomaly. Admittedly, it could seem like one. Luke, like any historian, naturally selects the events he sees as most significant, and this selectivity could create the impression that the first generation of the church was a breathless string of astonishing miracles, eloquent speeches, and evangelistic breakthroughs. A more careful reading reveals another side to things: the people who were not spared from death, the months of voyages where (to our knowledge) no miracles occurred, Paul's lengthy imprisonment and trial. Yet even if we take the miraculous high points and then turn to the Epistles, we find—perhaps to our surprise—that they reflect strikingly similar expectations of the Christian life (although, alas, without the teleportations).

The believers in Rome are urged to use the gifts, or *charismata*, they have been given, including prophesying in proportion to their faith.[2] The Galatians have such a clear experience of the Spirit working miracles among them, whatever those miracles were, that Paul can use it to ground his argument about faith and works of Torah.[3] The Ephesians are commanded to be filled with the Spirit rather

---

2 Romans 12:6.
3 Galatians 3:5.

than getting drunk on wine, and to pray in the Spirit at all times.[4] The Thessalonians are told not to quench the Spirit or despise prophecies, but rather to test everything and hold fast to what is good.[5] Timothy is encouraged to wage spiritual warfare according to prophecies made about him.[6] Hebrews appeals to the evidence of signs, wonders, miracles, and the gifts of the Holy Spirit, in order to warn a congregation on the verge of backsliding.[7] James urges the sick to call the elders for anointing with oil and proclaims that the prayer of faith will heal them.[8] If Acts gives us the headlines and the heroes, the Epistles demonstrate, almost incidentally, just how widespread the gifts of the Spirit were in the early church.

Not just the gifts of the Spirit, either: Paul takes it for granted that his readers will share his *experience* of the Holy Spirit. He has never visited the church in Rome, but he is absolutely certain that they have experienced the Spirit of adoption crying out "Abba! Father!" from deep within them, simply because having received the Spirit is what makes a person a believer.[9] He knows that they share his experience of the Spirit praying for them with groans that cannot be expressed in words.[10] He assumes that believers know what he is talking about when he tells them to be filled with the Spirit or pray in the Spirit or sing spiritual songs.[11] He knows Christians have experienced the Spirit shedding abroad the love of God into their hearts and sealing them for future glory, like a deposit, like a guarantee. Reminding them of this fact becomes his main way of giving believers assurance.[12]

The Spirit, for Paul, is at the center of Christian discipleship. Repeatedly, where modern evangelicals might be inclined to point people first to the Bible, or the gospel—pray in the Bible, rejoice in the gospel, be led by the Bible, find assurance in the gospel, experience

---

4 Ephesians 5:18; 6:18.
5 1 Thessalonians 5:19–21.
6 1 Timothy 1:18.
7 Hebrews 2:3–4.
8 James 5:14–15.
9 Romans 8:9, 14–17; Galatians 4:1–7.
10 Romans 8:26–27.
11 Ephesians 5:18–21; Colossians 3:16.
12 Romans 5:5; 2 Corinthians 1:21–22; 5:5; Ephesians 1:13–14.

God's love through the Bible, keep in step with the gospel, and so on—Paul points people first to the Spirit.[13] The chief actor in the sanctification of the believer is not a message, but a Messenger: a person who can be grieved or honored, not just a word that can be rejected or believed. The third person of the Trinity, for Paul, was a dynamic, experienced reality.[14]

It is abundantly clear from the New Testament that this expectation, both of spiritual gifts and spiritual experience, was for ordinary believers and not just for the apostles. I say that partly because of the very matter-of-fact way in which Paul refers to both miracles and experiences in the lives of his converts, as we have seen, and partly because of the named individuals, like Stephen, Philip, Ananias, and Agabus, who work miracles without being apostles. But I also say it because of the (otherwise inexplicable) phenomenon of anonymous miracles. This point is often missed in discussions of this subject, but it deserves a moment's reflection.

Miracle stories typically point to miracle workers. Outside of Scripture, miracles usually highlight the unique powers of the individual performing them; in the Old Testament and the Gospels, they frequently validate a person's God-given ministry and message. At Pentecost, however, things change somewhat. On several occasions, certainly, the apostles are specifically identified as the ones through whom many signs and wonders are performed. But in a number of other texts, miraculous gifts are given to ordinary members of the church: people so ordinary that not only are they not apostles, they are not even named. Of the one hundred and twenty people who spill out into the streets speaking in unlearned languages, we know the names of at most twenty, and none of them are regarded as having worked the miracle—rather, as Peter is at pains to point out, it is the ascended Jesus who is responsible for pouring out what people

---

13 Ultimately there is no dichotomy here, of course, since the Spirit speaks through the Scriptures—but there remains a difference of emphasis. The Bible is authoritative because of God the Holy Spirit, not vice versa.

14 The classic study of this theme remains that of Gordon Fee, *God's Empowering Presence* (Peabody: Hendrickson, 1994).

now see and hear.[15] The same is true a few chapters later when an unknown number of Cornelius's relatives and friends begin speaking in languages.[16] The twelve disciples of John the Baptist who end up prophesying and speaking in languages are never named.[17] Neither are Philip's four daughters who prophesied.[18] Neither are the elders who prophesied over Timothy and, apparently, imparted his gift to him.[19] Miraculous gifts, in the New Testament, are not just for the apostles or even just for prominent, named individuals. They are for ordinary, anonymous, regular people.

This is without mentioning 1 Corinthians. If the apostles are at one end of the impressive Christianity spectrum, the church in Corinth are at the other. Not because of their very ordinary backgrounds—although, as Paul reminds them, that too—but because they seem to have worked their way through the entire body of Christian doctrine and praxis, and made a pig's ear of all of it. There is division, not unity, about virtually everything: leadership, baptism, marriage, idol food, spiritual gifts, eschatology. The foolishness of the cross has been traded for the wisdom of worldly rhetoric and self-important boasting. A prominent individual is living incestuously, and the church is proud of it. Church members are suing each other. Some are visiting prostitutes. Some are participating in idolatrous worship. Corporate gatherings are a weekly debacle and do more harm than good: license-flaunting dress codes, drunkenness at the Lord's Supper, self-indulgent spirituality, total chaos. Even the future resurrection of believers is being denied. We quote the letter at weddings—"If I speak in the tongues of men and of angels, but have not love, I am a noisy gong or a clanging cymbal"[20]—but it's easy to forget that Paul wasn't

15 Acts 2:32–33.
16 Acts 10:44–48.
17 Acts 19:1–7.
18 Acts 21:9.
19 1 Timothy 4:14.
20 1 Corinthians 13:1.

speaking hypothetically; he was talking about the church in Corinth. Frankly, it is hard to imagine a church less apparently qualified to receive miraculous gifts.

Yet there they all are. "You are not lacking in any gift," Paul tells them in his (breathtakingly confident) opening paragraph, "as you wait for the revealing of our Lord Jesus Christ, who will sustain you to the end, guiltless in the day of our Lord Jesus Christ."[21] You are not lacking in any *charismata*. Collectively, you have *all* of them. And this to a church of nobodies, bunglers, squabblers, and boasters. It almost beggars belief.

It is not until chapter twelve that we start to get an idea of what these spiritual gifts are.[22] Paul, eager that the Corinthians not be "uninformed" on the subject, explains that "to each is given the manifestation of the Spirit for the common good," and then mentions a bunch of examples: the utterance of wisdom, the utterance of knowledge, faith, gifts of healing, the working of miracles, prophecy, the ability to distinguish between spirits, various kinds of tongues, and the interpretation of tongues.[23] We can be fairly sure that this is not an exhaustive list.[24] Nothing Paul says here indicates that there is anything anomalous, or weird, about the fact that the Corinthians have these gifts. Far from it: he grounds it all in their conversion (12:2–3), the Trinity (vv. 4–6), the common good of the church (vv. 7–11), the gift of the Spirit to all believers (vv. 12–13), and the interdependence of the church body (vv. 14–31).

So whatever else we may say about the experience and gifts of the Spirit, it is clear that to be a Christian in Greece in the AD 50s meant at least five things. One: you had already been baptized, or drenched, in one Spirit into one body. Two: you had been given one

---

21 1 Corinthians 1:7.

22 Although Paul briefly refers to singleness, and by implication also marriage, as a *charisma* from God (7:7).

23 1 Corinthians 12:7–10.

24 The fact that the list is not exhaustive seems clear from a comparison with other lists in Paul, including 1 Corinthians 12:27–30 (apostles, prophets, teachers, miracles, gifts of healing, helping, administrating, various kinds of tongues) and Romans 12:6–8 (prophesying, serving, teaching, exhorting, giving, leading, showing mercy).

Spirit to drink. Taken together, these two images are highly experiential—if you are drenched, or have a drink, you really know it—and suggest that the experience of the Spirit is both initiatory and ongoing.[25] Three: you had been given some gifts (or manifestations) of the Spirit for the common good, whether gifts of wisdom, knowledge or prophecy, healing or miracles, languages or their interpretation, faith or distinguishing between spirits, or whatever else. Four: you had not been given all of these gifts, and nor were any gifts common to all believers. Five: as a result, you were called to serve the other members of the body with your gifts, just as you needed them to serve you with theirs. That meant you had to see your gifts as a means of exercising love for others, rather than a means of spiritual gratification or showing off, a point which Paul then develops at some length, both in principle (1 Corinthians 13) and in practice (chapter 14).

It is worth pointing out that those five things present challenges to certain forms of charismatic Christianity today. They problematize readings of Paul that identify two types of believer: those who drink of and are drenched in the Spirit (Pentecostals or charismatics), and those who don't and aren't (everyone else).[26] They challenge the use of any one gift as a shibboleth to mark out those who are truly full of the Spirit, as Pentecostals have traditionally done with the gift of languages. They show that the gift of healing is a *gift*, given to some in particular measure, rather than something that all believers would be able to do on demand if they simply had enough faith or prayed a certain way or adopted a particular technique. In centering on the metaphor of a human body, and the need to love and serve one another, they also call all believers to repent of using the gifts in service of sectarianism, individualism, division, or pride, let alone the greed and falsehood that can be found in so much "prosperity" Christianity.

---

25 This combination of initiatory and ongoing experience is also apparent from the accounts of filling with the Spirit in Acts (2:4; 4:8, 31; 9:17; 13:9, 52), Paul's exhortation to the Ephesians (5:18), and Jesus's language in John's gospel (cp. 4:14 and 7:37–39).
26 An influential example of this sort of reading can be found in the expository sermons of Martyn Lloyd-Jones on Romans (8:14–17) and Ephesians (1:13–14).

At the same time, they reveal two striking features of the New Testament church. Unless the Corinthians were a strange anomaly in this respect—and, as we have seen, both Acts and the other epistles indicate that they were not—normal Christianity involved emphatic encounters with the person of the Holy Spirit, such that metaphors like "filling," "drinking," and "drenching" seemed appropriate, and an expectation of spiritual gifts like prophecy, healing, languages, or miracles. Neither of these things were reserved for the superstars or the key leaders or the eyewitnesses of the resurrection. They were part of the everyday experience of ordinary Christians, everywhere.

So were angels and demons.

This might seem too obvious to need mentioning. After all, spiritual beings appear in virtually every book of the Bible, whether they are called angels, the sons of God, the divine council, archangels, cherubim, seraphim, Satan, the devil, demons, principalities, powers, thrones, dominions, rulers, authorities, spiritual forces of evil, strongholds, or anything else. When they do, they are not mere metaphors for existentialist or spiritual struggle, or whatever patronizing modernist claptrap might be in vogue at the moment; they are presented as real spiritual beings with genuine agency in the world of space and time. In the world of the New Testament, angels and demons are as real, ordinary, and commonplace as animals.

Then again, perhaps this point does need to be mentioned after all. Everybody reads Scripture in light of their experience, and the reality is that an awful lot of contemporary churches operate with no expectation whatsoever of angelic or demonic interaction with our world. Consequently, even when we read about it in the Bible (let alone in church history), we either don't notice it at all or read the relevant stories through a different lens altogether.[27] Pauline scholars

---

27 For a strident, if not always persuasive, account of this phenomenon, see Michael Heiser, *The Unseen Realm: Recovering the Supernatural Worldview of the Bible* (Bellingham: Lexham, 2015), especially parts I and II.

take the language of thrones and authorities and apply it to empires and social structures, as opposed to angels or demons.[28] Preachers may speculate on whether demonization in the Gospels is "really" a matter of epilepsy or schizophrenia. Pastors can stress the importance of fighting sin or idolatry or the flesh or the world, but not the devil. Counselors and therapists might emphasize that our struggle is not against principalities and powers, but against neurons and chemicals, flesh and blood. As for the passages in which the preaching of the gospel is accompanied by the driving out of demons, they are more likely to be met with an embarrassed cough or a baffled silence than with a summons to go and do likewise.

This is not always, or even usually, from bad motives. We genuinely seem to find it hard to believe in both angels and anesthetics at the same time. Scientific explanations, with all their logical tidiness and predictive power, seem to render unnecessary the need for spiritual ones, and there are obviously all sorts of conditions that can be treated with prescriptions as well as with prayer. On the other hand, especially in WEIRD[29] societies, this "as well as" can quickly become "in preference to," and ultimately "instead of." The result is a spirituality that is functionally naturalistic. As C. S. Lewis expressed so winsomely in *The Screwtape Letters*, it is tremendously helpful for demons when we disregard their agency altogether and act as if we have grown out of believing in them. The greatest trick the devil ever pulled was convincing the world he didn't exist.[30]

A brief glance at the history of the church in previous centuries, or even at the parts of the world where the gospel is making the greatest impact in this one, will expose how unique this phenomenon is to late modern, mostly white, European Christianity. If you read a random sample of patristic writings, you will quickly notice it: the church fathers believed not only in the existence of angels and

---

28 The problem here is not applying such language to earthly empires, but failing to apply it to spiritual beings.

29 WEIRD stands for Western, Educated, Industrialized, Rich, and Democratic.

30 Compare Graham Greene's comment in *The End of the Affair* (New York: Penguin, 2004), 47: "I have never understood why people who can swallow the enormous improbability of a personal God boggle at a personal Devil."

demons, but in their agency, their power, their influence and inten-
tionality, and they talked about it all the time. The Athanasius who
confronted Arius over the divinity of Christ, and shaped the canon of
Scripture that we have to this day, is also the Athanasius who wrote
this of St. Anthony (360):

> The demons made such a racket that the whole place was
> shaken, knocking over the four walls of the tomb; they came
> in droves, taking the form of all kinds of monstrous beasts
> and hideous reptiles. . . . They all were making a terrible noise.
> Groaning in pain, St. Anthony faced the demons, laughing: "If
> you had any power, only one of you would be enough to kill
> me; but the Lord has taken away your strength, so you want to
> frighten me by your number. The proof of your powerlessness is
> that you are reduced to taking the form of senseless animals. If
> you have any power against me, come on, attack me! But if you
> cannot do anything, why torment yourselves unnecessarily?
> My faith in God is my defense against you." But all of a sudden a
> bright light illuminated the tomb; at that moment, the demons
> vanished.[31]

Augustine's *City of God* (426), hardly a marginal text in the
Western canon, contains four books on the subject of angels and
demons, out of a total of twenty-two.[32] Spiritual beings occupy one
fifth of the first part of Thomas Aquinas's *Summa Theologica* (1265–
74), including a fascinating discussion of "whether men are assailed
by the demons" and "whether demons can lead men astray by means
of real miracles."[33] (Spoiler alert: yes, and yes.) Luther's wranglings
with demons, and often with the devil himself, are sufficiently vivid
to make the most dyed-in-the-wool Pentecostal raise their eyebrows.
Angelic and demonic beings are ubiquitous in Eastern and Western
painting, which will be immediately obvious to anyone who has ever

---

31 Athanasius, *Life of St Anthony*, 9–10.
32 Augustine, *City of God*, Books IX–XII.
33 Thomas Aquinas, *Summa Theologica*, first part, Q114 (see also Q50–64, 106–13).

walked around an art gallery for a few minutes. All of which is to say that, from a historical perspective, let alone a global one, the relative disregard for angels and demons amongst evangelical Christians in WEIRD cultures is, in a word, weird.

One brief story may illustrate the point. In Acts 12, Peter is broken out of prison by an angel. The Jerusalem church, who have been interceding for him, are gathered in prayer at Mary's house, and suddenly Peter shows up at the door. When the servant girl Rhoda goes to let everyone know the good news, the church dismisses her as mad: "You are out of your mind. . . . It is his angel!"[34] Of the many intriguing things about this incident, the one that strikes me is this: the early church considered it more likely that an angel had just appeared at the door, than that Peter had just escaped from prison. *No, it's not Peter, you silly girl; it's only his angel.* Is there a church in the Western world today where that would be considered the more likely explanation? If not, what does that tell us? Are not angels ministering spirits, sent to serve those who inherit salvation?[35]

Admittedly, it is entirely possible for a church to affirm the existence and agency of angels and demons, and live as if they interact with us on a daily basis, yet at the same time to teach that all the miraculous gifts have ceased. Martin Luther saw no inconsistency between giving traveling fanatical prophets from Zwickau a punch on the nose by day and fighting the devil by night. It is equally possible for a church to hold the opposite: that angels and demons do not interact with us any more, for whatever reason, but that the miraculous gifts continue. But it would probably be fair to say that today, both of these positions are uncommon, and that generally speaking, the more charismatic a believer is, the more likely they are to recognize the activity of angels and demons in daily life and to pray accordingly. (They are also more likely, at least in Protestant circles, to express

---

34 Acts 12:15.
35 Hebrews 1:14. Interestingly, Acts 12 concludes with a third angelic story, in which Herod is struck down by the angel of the Lord for accepting blasphemous praise. The frequency with which angels appear in Acts may help us understand why the Jerusalem church jumped to the conclusion they did.

the gospel in terms of Christ's cosmic victory over the devil and the forces of evil.)

You can see why. A world in which demons continue to act is more likely to be a world in which Christians are called to cast them out in the name of Jesus. This in turn is more likely to be a world in which the gift of distinguishing between spirits continues and in which there is a smaller gap between the praxis of the New Testament church and that of the contemporary church. The appearance of angels, likewise, narrows the distance between the apostolic age and the digital age and leads us to expect that the miraculous phenomena that accompanied the preaching of the gospel then will continue to accompany it now.

Flipping things around, it is also easy to see how a rejection of miraculous gifts could lead to a rejection of many, if not all, modern miracles as spurious, which in turn could lead to a rejection of many, if not all, accounts of supernatural phenomena as spurious, including appearances of angels and demons. When this happens in a church culture that is doubly suspicious of miraculous claims already—driven both by secularist anti-supernaturalism, and by a centuries-old Protestant skepticism of Roman Catholic superstition—the pressure to treat angels and demons as spooky, or mere figments of gullible imaginations, could become irresistible.

I stress: none of this proves that the miraculous gifts continue or that cessationism (the belief that the miraculous gifts ceased at the end of the New Testament period) is incoherent. At most, it proves that *if* angels and demons continue to operate in the world, as the church has long insisted they do, then *one particular type* of cessationist argument—that miraculous phenomena in general only occur in specific phases of world history, and have not done so since the apostolic age—is incoherent. Nevertheless, it provides important context for the wider discussion about miracles and gifts. And it suggests that when African Christians talk about their encounters with angels or demons, and North American Christians respond with an eye-roll, the former are closer to both biblical and historic Christianity than the latter.

🔥 🔥 🔥

So the pages of the New Testament reveal a charismatic church, characterized by an experience both of the person of the Holy Spirit—one
that could be described in very tangible ways, including drenching,
filling, drinking, crying out "Abba!" and so forth—and of angels and
demons, languages and interpretation, prophecy and teaching, healing and miracles. No distinction was made between "miraculous
gifts" and "ordinary gifts" or between "gifts that could only be used
by apostles" and "gifts that could be used by anyone" or anything
like that. Nor, despite occasional claims to the contrary, does the
New Testament suggest that miracles gradually tapered off or faded
away over time; if anything, the miracles described at the end of Acts
(around AD 60), when Paul survives a snake bite, cures a man of dys-
entery, and then heals an entire island, are even more dramatic and
widespread than those described at the beginning of it (around AD
30).[36] What Paul told the Corinthians seems to have been true of the
early church in general: "You are not lacking any gift, as you wait for
the revealing of our Lord Jesus Christ." Biblical Christianity was charismatic Christianity.[37]

The claim I am making here, however, is not just that the
miraculous gifts were given throughout the New Testament period.
That much should be uncontroversial. I am also arguing that they
continue to be given today—prophecy, languages, interpretation,
teaching, miracles, healing, and the rest—and that, like every good
gift that our Father gives us, they should be pursued as a result.[38] Put

---

36 Acts 28:1–10.
37 This is acknowledged beautifully in perhaps the best cessationist book I have come across,
   namely Richard Gaffin, *Perspectives on Pentecost* (Phillipsburg: Presbyterian and Reformed,
   1979), 48: "Biblically speaking, 'charismatic' and 'Christian' are synonymous. The Christian life in
   its totality is (to be) a charismatic life. Christ's church as a *whole* is *the* charismatic movement."
38 Sharp-eyed readers will note that I have not included apostles in this list. There are three main
   reasons for that. (1) On the two occasions where Paul self-consciously lists the *pneumatika* or
   charismata that believers should use for the common good, he does not include apostleship
   among them (Romans 12:6–8; 1 Corinthians 12:4–11). When he mentions apostles in 1 Corinthians 12:27–31, he describes them as that which God has appointed in the church—as a

differently, I am arguing that Romans 12:6, 1 Corinthians 12:31, and 14:1 still apply: believers are urged to use, to be zealous for, to earnestly desire, and to strive for spiritual gifts. (This, we could mention in passing, is very different from being "open to" spiritual gifts if they happen to come along. I am "zealous for" time with my wife; if I said I was "open to" it, there would probably be consequences.) This much is highly controversial, of course, as a few minutes on the internet will quickly reveal.[39] Even so, I say it for three main reasons.

The first, perhaps surprisingly, is *historical.* That is, one of the best reasons to think the miraculous gifts continued is the fact that, according to many of the church fathers, they did. In the context of contemporary debates, this point is often lost, not least because the gift that has proved the most divisive in the last hundred years or so, namely the gift of languages, is the one over which the patristic evidence is least clear. Charismatics are also, to generalize for a moment, less interested in the fathers than many more conservative branches of Christianity, in part because our narrative is so often presented (unhelpfully) as a bold rediscovery of something the church had lost for nineteen centuries. As a result, cessationists have leaned into the historical evidence, and charismatics have leaned away from it, even

---

way of illustrating his point about the interdependence of the body—but not as an example of *pneumatika* or *charismata.* Ephesians 4:11, likewise, is not a list of gifts that individual Christians should aspire to; the gifts are individuals who have been given to the church by the risen Christ. (2) All interpreters recognize that the word *apostolos* is used in quite different ways in the New Testament, ranging from the very specific (the Twelve in Acts 1:26) to the very general (the unnamed brothers who collect the offering for the poor in 2 Corinthians 8:23). Clearly, the former *apostoloi* are unique to the first century, and the latter are not—in that sense we are all cessationists regarding the former, and we are all continuationists regarding the latter—which means that statements about the gift of apostle today require immediate clarification. For my own argument on the subject, see my "Apostle Apollos?" in *JETS* 56.2 (June 2013). (3) The *charismata* or *pneumatika* that Paul tells the Corinthians to be zealous for (1 Corinthians 12:31; 14:1) almost certainly do not include apostleship, and few (if any) interpreters have argued that they do (cf. 9:1–2; 15:8–9). This is not to say that Paul did not regard his apostleship as a grace-gift, since he clearly did (Romans 1:1–7); it is simply to say that it does not appear to be one of the gifts he urges his converts to pursue (1 Corinthians 12:31; 14:1) and to use (Romans 12:6). To include it here, therefore, would muddy the waters.

39 Probably the most forceful recent response to the charismatic case made here is that of John MacArthur, *Strange Fire: The Danger of Offending the Holy Spirit with Counterfeit Worship* (Nashville: Thomas Nelson, 2013).

though much of it indicates that the gifts continued (a position often called "continuationism").

Justin Martyr, the first great Christian apologist, put it bluntly in his *Dialogue with Trypho* (160):

> *For the prophetical gifts remain with us, even to the present time.* And hence you ought to understand that [the gifts] formerly among your nation have been transferred to us. And just as there were false prophets contemporaneous with your holy prophets, so are there now many false teachers among us, of whom our Lord forewarned us to beware.[40]

In more detail, here is Irenaeus of Lyon (180):

> Wherefore, also, those who are in truth His disciples, receiving grace from Him, do in His name perform [miracles], so as to promote the welfare of other men, according to the gift which each one has received from Him. For some do certainly and truly *drive out devils*, so that those who have thus been cleansed from *evil spirits* frequently both believe [in Christ], and join themselves to the Church. Others have foreknowledge of things to come: *they see visions, and utter prophetic expressions. Others still, heal the sick by laying their hands upon them,* and they are made whole. Yea, moreover, as I have said, *the dead even have been raised up,* and remained among us for many years. And what shall I more say? It is not possible to name the number of the gifts which the Church, [scattered] throughout the whole world, has received from God, in the name of Jesus Christ....[41]
>
> For this reason does the apostle declare, "We speak wisdom among them that are perfect," terming those persons "perfect" who have received the Spirit of God, and who through the Spirit of God do speak in all languages, as he used Himself

---

40 Justin Martyr, *Dialogue with Trypho* 82 (emphasis has been added to all the quotations in this section).

41 Irenaeus, *Against Heresies* 2.32.4.

also to speak. *In like manner we do also hear many brethren in the Church, who possess prophetic gifts, and who through the Spirit speak all kinds of languages, and bring to light for the general benefit the hidden things of men, and declare the mysteries of God*, whom also the apostle terms "spiritual," they being spiritual because they partake of the Spirit, and not because their flesh has been stripped off and taken away, and because they have become purely spiritual.[42]

Notice that the gifts mentioned here include prophecy, healing, and languages, the three most often argued to have ceased after the first century. Eusebius, the first great historian of the church, uses this excerpt to demonstrate that "various gifts remained among those who were worthy even until that time."[43]

In slightly more bombastic fashion, Tertullian of Carthage (208) throws down the gauntlet to the heretic Marcion, challenging him to produce the same sorts of spiritual gifts—visions, prophecies, interpretations of tongues—as the orthodox church can:

> Let Marcion then exhibit, as gifts of his god, some prophets, such as have not spoken by human sense, but with the Spirit of God, such as have both predicted things to come, and have made manifest the secrets of the heart; let him produce a psalm, a vision, a prayer—only let it be by the Spirit, in an ecstasy, that is, in a rapture, whenever an interpretation of tongues has occurred to him; let him show to me also, that any woman of boastful tongue in his community has ever prophesied from among those specially holy sisters of his. *Now all these signs (of spiritual gifts) are forthcoming from my side without any difficulty,* and they agree, too, with the rules, and the dispensations, and the instructions of the Creator.[44]

---

42 Irenaeus, *Against Heresies* 5.6.1.

43 Eusebius, *Ecclesiastical History* 5.7.1–6; cf. also 5.17.4, quoting Apollinaris: "for the apostle thought it necessary that the prophetic gift should continue in all the Church until the final coming."

44 Tertullian, *Against Marcion*, 5.8.

Forty years later (248), at the opposite end of the empire to Irenaeus, Origen of Alexandria argues:

We have to say, moreover, that the Gospel has a demonstration of its own, more divine than any established by Grecian dialectics. And this diviner method is called by the apostle the manifestation of the Spirit and of power: of the Spirit, on account of the prophecies, which are sufficient to produce faith in any one who reads them, especially in those things which relate to Christ; *and of power, because of the signs and wonders which we must* believe *to have been performed, both on many other grounds, and on this, that traces of them are still preserved among those who regulate their lives by the precepts of the Gospel*. . . . And there are still preserved among Christians traces of that Holy Spirit which appeared in the form of a dove. *They expel evil spirits, and perform many cures, and foresee certain events*, according to the will of the Logos. . . . And the name of *Jesus* can still remove distractions from the minds of men, and expel demons, and also take away diseases.[45]

He later elaborates:

And *some give evidence of their having received through this faith a marvellous power by the cures which they perform*, revoking no other name over those who need their help than that of the God of all things, and of Jesus, along with a mention of his history. For by these means we too have seen many persons freed from grievous calamities, and from distractions of mind, and madness, and countless other ills, which could be cured neither by men nor devils. . . . God desired to commend the doctrine of Jesus as a doctrine which was to save mankind, and which was

---

45 Origen, *Against Celsus* 1.2, 46, 67; cf. also 2:8; 3:3; 7.8; 8:58. Origen is sometimes quoted in support of cessationism, but it seems clear from *Against Celsus* that he regarded miraculous signs and gifts, including prophecy, healings, and the casting out of demons, to have diminished since the time of the apostles, but not to have ceased.

based, indeed, upon the apostles as foundations of the rising edifice of Christianity, but which increased in magnitude also in *the succeeding ages, in which not a few cures are wrought in the name of* Jesus, *and certain other manifestations of no small moment have taken place.*[46]

A century after that, we find Basil the Great describing the work of the Spirit in striking terms:

Through the rebirth from above . . . the Spirit enlightens all, *inspires prophets*, gives wisdom to lawmakers, consecrates priests, empowers kings, perfects the just, exalts the prudent, *is active in gifts of healing*, gives life to the dead, frees those in bondage, turns foreigners into adopted sons.[47]

Around the same time (350), Cyril of Jerusalem was catechizing new disciples like this:

And though He is One in nature, yet many are the virtues which by the will of God and in the Name of Christ He works. For He employs the tongue of one man for wisdom; *the soul of another He enlightens by Prophecy; to another He gives power to drive away devils*; to another He gives to interpret the divine Scriptures. He strengthens one man's self-command; He teaches another the way to give alms; another He teaches to fast and discipline himself; another he teaches to despise the things of the body; another He trains for martyrdom: diverse in different men, yet not diverse from Himself, as it is written.[48]

Another century later, Augustine dedicated an entire chapter of his *City of God* (426) to the continuation of miracles, indignant

---

46 Origen, *Against Celsus* 3.24, 28.

47 Basil, Homily 3, translated in Mark DelCogliano, *St Basil the Great: On Christian Doctrine and Practice* (Yonkers: St. Vladimir's Seminary Press, 2013), 238.

48 Cyril of Jerusalem, *Catechetical Lectures* 16.12.

at the suggestion that they ceased with the apostles. He claimed to have witnessed a number himself, and lists an extraordinary range of healings from blindness, rectal fistula, breast cancer, gout, paralysis, hernia, demonization, and even death.[49] Augustine's testimony is particularly significant because of his enormous impact on the Western Church: it would not be an exaggeration to say that *City of God* was the most influential book in Europe for the next thousand years. When we add his comments to those of Justin, Irenaeus, Tertullian, Origen, Eusebius, Basil, and Cyril—and I am deliberately omitting a number of more controversial references—we have a huge spread chronologically (from the mid-second century to the early fifth), charismatically (prophecy, visions, languages, interpretations, exorcisms, healings, miracles), and geographically (in the far East and far West of the empire, and north and south of the Mediterranean).[50] In other words, the patristic period was far more charismatic than is often recognized.

There are, admittedly, a few references in the post-Nicene fathers to the disappearance of some, or even all, of the gifts. Augustine, before writing his spirited defense of miracles in *City of God*, argued that the gift of languages had served its purpose and then finished.[51] John Chrysostom (349–407) spoke of the loss of the miraculous gifts somewhat wistfully, comparing it to a woman who used to be wealthy but now retains only the symbols of her former prosperity.[52] But we should be careful not to use passages like this to filter out all the other evidence. Late fourth- and early fifth-century claims that particular gifts no longer operate, even when accompanied by a theological rationale, do not trump testimony from the previous three centuries that they do, despite the conversation-stopping finality

---

49 Augustine, *City of God* 22.8.

50 More controversial references would include Didache 11 (since its date is unclear), Mark 16:9–20 (since its authorship is unclear), and Tertullian's defense of the Montanists (as they were eventually seen as heterodox).

51 E.g., Augustine, *Homilies on the First Epistle of John* 6.10.

52 Chrysostom, *Homilies on First Corinthians* 29.1; 36.7. There is also an ambiguous comment from Theodoret of Cyrus (393–466) about the visible signs of grace "in former times" and the fact that grace in his day "may not take the same form as it did in those days."

with which they are sometimes parked on cessationist websites.[53] If I was to write today that nobody has fired a cannon since the death of Cromwell, and then you were to read descriptions of cannons being fired from various eighteenth- and nineteenth-century historians, you would be well-advised to read my argument through the lens of their testimony, not the other way around.

In other words, if we want to find out whether the miraculous gifts continued after the apostles died, we should ask the people who lived after the apostles died. On balance, based on the evidence we have, the answer is yes.[54]

The second reason for pursuing the gifts today is *hermeneutical*. Put simply, this is the principle that explicit New Testament instructions to Christians should be followed, unless there is a clear reason from the context why they should not be. This presumption of obedience, it seems to me, should be a fairly uncontroversial rule of thumb for anyone who follows Jesus; we are under the same covenant as our first-century brothers and sisters, and as such, we should assume that what the apostles taught them, they would also teach us. In other words, the burden of proof should always be on the person who says we don't have to obey an apostolic instruction, rather than on the person who says we do. If we flip that round, we quickly end up in pick-and-choose territory.

Sometimes this burden of proof can be met. No Christians in history have made it their business to go to Troas and look for Paul's coat,

---

53 It is also worth reflecting on the reasons for such claims of cessation in their historical contexts, from Judaism to Montanism, and on into Aristotelian metaphysics (Aquinas), Roman Catholic piety (the Reformers), and the Enlightenment (through to today); see Jon Mark Ruthven, *On the Cessation of the Charismata: The Protestant Polemic on Post-Biblical Miracles* (Sheffield: Sheffield Academic Press, 1993).

54 Historical studies show that the sign gifts were also practiced in medieval Europe, including languages, healings, miracles, and prophecy; see, e.g., Stanley Burgess, *The Holy Spirit: Medieval Roman Catholic and Reformation Traditions* (Grand Rapids: Baker, 1994), introduction: the miraculous gifts "were referred to constantly in medieval hagiographic literature (that is, accounts of the lives of the saints)—indeed, so frequently and so uncritically that many modern scholars have come to discredit all such accounts. In doing so, however, skeptics have failed to consider that these reports of the paranormal were believed by virtually all pre-Renaissance Christians." See also his more recent *Christian Peoples of the Spirit: A Documentary History of Pentecostal Spirituality from the Early Church to the Present* (New York: NYU Press, 2011).

for instance, because it is obvious from Paul's letter that his request only applied to Timothy.[55] Nor have we followed Jesus's instruction to "go nowhere among the gentiles," because it is clear from the wider context of Matthew's gospel that this instruction was for the specific period before Jesus's ascension and does not apply to subsequent generations.[56] In these cases, and various others, the limited scope of the instruction is clearly indicated in the text. But if there is no such indication in the text—if an instruction is given without being clearly confined in scope in some way—we should assume it also applies to us.

This has big implications when it comes to the pursuit of the gifts. "Zealously desire spiritual gifts," Paul says.[57] Or, fourteen verses earlier, "Zealously desire the greater gifts."[58] Or, later in the same discussion, "Zealously desire to prophesy, and do not forbid speaking in tongues."[59] Or, as part of his exhortation to humility in Romans, "Having gifts that differ according to the grace given to us, let us use them: if prophecy, in proportion to our faith."[60] Or, in his conclusion to 1 Thessalonians, "Do not quench the Spirit. Do not despise prophecies, but test everything; hold fast what is good."[61] Sometimes the debate over the pursuit of the gifts can look like a no-score-draw, with continuationists pointing out that the New Testament never says the gifts will cease, and cessationists responding that it never says they won't, either. But in light of the hermeneutical principle we would normally use—and I tend to call it the Presumption Of Obedience, although I am not wild about the acronym—the reality is different. Our default setting, if you like, should be one of obeying these passages, and eagerly desiring spiritual gifts, unless a clear case to the contrary can be made from the text.

---

55 2 Timothy 4:13.
56 Matthew 10:5; cf., e.g., Matthew 28:19–20.
57 1 Corinthians 14:1.
58 1 Corinthians 12:31.
59 1 Corinthians 14:39; cf. also 14:31: "For you can all prophesy one by one, so that all may learn and all be encouraged."
60 Romans 12:6.
61 1 Thessalonians 5:19–21.

Two ways of making this case—that, although there are apostolic instructions to pursue the miraculous gifts, we should not do so—are particularly common. The first relates to the "low quality" of contemporary miracles. Jesus and the apostles (so the argument goes) healed totally, instantaneously, and irrevocably; modern healings are rarely, if ever, like that. The languages at Pentecost were earthly and comprehensible; the modern gift of languages, usually, is not. Agabus accurately prophesied a famine; modern prophecies are more hit and miss. Evidently, there are a variety of responses that a charismatic could make to this. Such comments usually come from within a Western, functionally materialist society, which misses out on much of the global, and often far more charismatic, picture. Jesus himself didn't always heal instantaneously.[62] There are actually far more instantaneous and dramatic miracles these days than we may realize.[63] Tongues in Paul's letters were probably a prayer language rather than an earthly language.[64] Paul didn't heal everyone—in at least one case, he wasn't healed himself—and arguably Jesus didn't either.[65]

The best response, however, is to grant the central point, and then show that it does not matter. Yes, the apostles were more successful

---

62 Mark 8:22–26.

63 Craig Keener, *Miracles: The Credibility of the New Testament Accounts*, 2 vols (Grand Rapids: Baker, 2012).

64 The gift of languages on the day of Pentecost and the gift of languages in the church at Corinth are almost certainly different. This is true whether or not we see Paul as alluding to the difference in his famous comment about "the tongues of men, and of angels." The former were immediately understood by those who heard; the latter required interpretation. The former demonstrated blessing, as those who speak other languages understand, in reversal of the curse of Babel; the latter demonstrated judgment, as those who speak other languages do not understand, in fulfilment of Isaiah. The former is assumed to function like prophecy by Peter; the latter is explicitly differentiated from prophecy by Paul. The former had a declarative, even evangelistic, purpose, and is aimed at people: "We hear them telling in our own tongues the mighty works of God" (Acts 2:11). The latter is described in terms of prayer, song and thanksgiving, and is aimed at God. The purpose of the former is the edification of the hearer; the purpose of the latter, if there is no interpreter, is the edification of the speaker. The two are, therefore, highly likely to be different in form. If Paul was addressing the use of the Pentecost-style gift of languages in Corinth, I suggest, he went about it in a very strange way. For the opposing case, see Thomas Schreiner, *Spiritual Gifts: What They Are and Why They Matter* (Nashville: B&H, 2018), 125–29.

65 2 Timothy 4:20; Galatians 5:13–14 (cf. the more ambiguous case of 2 Corinthians 12:1–10); John 5:1–9.

at healing and prophecy than we are. There is, indeed, a discrepancy between our experience and what is described in the New Testament. But the apostles were also far more successful at evangelism. And church planting. And leadership. And cross-cultural mission. And church discipline. And teaching. And standing firm under persecution. And handling disappointment. Yet in none of these cases do we conclude that the gulf is so wide, their "success" so much greater than ours, that to tell people how to share the gospel or teach or lead more effectively, is to encourage people to be satisfied with sub-biblical Christianity. Rather, we acknowledge the disparity and seek to learn from it. What did they do? How did they do it? What can we learn? What are we missing? Which contemporaries of ours is God using in this area at the moment? What can we learn from them? The same, surely, should apply to the miraculous gifts.

The other main way of making the cessationist case, and by far the stronger one, is built on the perceived tension, or incompatibility, between ongoing prophetic revelation and a closed New Testament canon.[66] (1) Old Testament prophecy, it is argued, was revelatory, foundational and infallible, and (2) New Testament prophecy is no different (Ephesians 2:20 is crucial here). (3) But with the death of the apostles and the closure of the New Testament canon this kind of foundational, infallible revelation has stopped being given (and claims to the contrary would inevitably reopen the canon, whether in the form of papal pronouncements, new inspired texts, or whatever). (4) Therefore the gift of prophecy has ceased. (5) Therefore the gift of languages, which functions very much like prophecy in 1 Corinthians 14, has also ceased. In most versions of this argument, (6) healing and miracles—which are given to confirm the validity of the message when it is first proclaimed—have ceased as well.

But notice how many things need to be granted for this argument to work. We need to know that all prophecy in the Old

---

66 For a succinct, gracious, and carefully argued version of this argument, see Schreiner, *Spiritual Gifts*, 93–146, 155–69 (though Schreiner is more cautious about argument [6], and calls his view a "nuanced cessationism").

Testament was infallible divine revelation.[67] We need to know that all prophecy in the New Testament period was also infallible divine revelation, the purpose of which was to establish the foundation of the church (because if any of it was not, then the door would be open for subsequent prophecy that did not conflict with the completion of Scripture).[68] We need to know that the gift of languages, properly interpreted, was also foundational and infallible revelation (for the same reason).[69] We need to know that the only purpose of healing and

---

67 For a number of fascinating reasons to doubt this—from an Old Testament professor at a conservative Presbyterian seminary, no less!—see Iain M. Duguid, "What Kind of Prophecy Continues? Defining the Differences between Continuationism and Cessationism," in John Frame, Wayne Grudem, and John Hughes (ed.), *Redeeming the Life of the Mind: Essays in Honor of Vern Poythress* (Wheaton: Crossway, 2017), chapter 7. Duguid highlights a number of instances where the word *prophet* or *prophesying* is used, yet "there is no suggestion of anyone listening to or being instructed by authoritative pronouncements"; rather, the person in view may be engaged in prayer, ecstatic speech, leading worship, or writing court history, and in such cases "prophecy functions not to convey divinely inspired information but to identify divinely indwelt individuals" (e.g. Genesis 20:7; Numbers 11:25–29; 1 Samuel 10:6; 19:20–23; 1 Kings 18:4; 2 Kings 2:3; 4:38; 6:1; 9:1; 17:13; 1 Chronicles 25:1–3; 29:29; 2 Chronicles 9:29; 12:15; 13:22).

68 Clearly this is the role of prophecy that Paul is referring to in Ephesians (2:20; 3:5), but it is far from clear that this is its only purpose. In 1 Corinthians 14 alone, we hear of prophecy being given to encourage, console, and edify other believers in the local church (14:3), bring unbelievers under conviction (14:24), witness to the presence of the Holy Spirit in the assembly (14:25), and enable the congregation to learn and be encouraged (14:31). It remains difficult to read 1 Corinthians 14 if we assume that Paul is speaking of infallible, foundational revelation throughout (with numerous Corinthian prophets chipping in, such that they had to be limited to two or three per meeting, often talking over each other, with their prophecies weighed by those sitting down, and none of it ever recorded or transmitted to another church), and there is a broad scholarly consensus that he is not. Nor do we have any indication that every instance of prophecy in Acts, some of which are not recorded at all, represented infallible and foundational revelation (11:27–30; 19:6; 21:9; compare also 21:10–11 and 21:33 on the question of who "bound" Paul); the same is true for the personal prophecy we find in the Pastoral Letters (1 Timothy 1:18; 4:14). For a better working definition of prophecy in Pauline theology, see Anthony Thiselton's *The First Epistle to the Corinthians* (Grand Rapids: Eerdmans, 2002), 956–65, 1087–94, especially at 965: "Prophecy, as a gift of the Holy Spirit, combines pastoral insight into the needs of persons, communities, and situations with the ability to address these with a God-given utterance or longer discourse (whether unprompted or prepared with judgment, decision and rational reflection) leading to challenge or comfort, judgment, or consolation, but ultimately building up the addressees. . . . While the speaker believes that such utterances or discourses come from the Holy Spirit, mistakes can be made, and since believers, including ministers or prophets, remain humanly fallible, claims to prophecy must be weighed and tested." This has, quite rightly, become a standard definition in the secondary literature; see, e.g., David Garland, *Baker Exegetical Commentary on the New Testament, 1 Corinthians* (Grand Rapids: Baker, 2003), 583; Roy Ciampa and Brian Rosner, *The First Letter to the Corinthians* (Grand Rapids: Eerdmans, 2010), 581.

69 This is an even more difficult case to make, since it faces all the problems we saw in the previ-

miracle gifts was to confirm the validity of the message when it was first proclaimed (because if they served any other purpose that might still apply today, then they may have continued).[70] And we need to be confident enough of these things to reassure people that in spite of Paul's instruction to pursue the *charismata*, we shouldn't.[71] Each of these steps faces its own difficulties; accepting all of them, despite my respect and affection for my cessationist friends, is beyond me.

Having said that, it is interesting that much of the debate here is about terminology, rather than reality. The terminology matters, of course, otherwise I would not be writing this; you can either exhort people in your congregation to earnestly desire prophecy, or you can't. But the difference may not be as large as it seems. As an example, here is a remarkable comment from Charles Spurgeon. It comes straight after his account of telling a shoemaker, whom he had never met, exactly how much money he had pilfered the previous week:

> I could tell as many as a *dozen* similar cases in which I pointed
> at somebody in the hall without having the slightest knowledge
> of the person, or any idea that what I said was right, except that
> I believed I was moved by the Spirit to say it; and so striking
> has been my description, that the persons have gone away, and

---

ous point, in addition to the fact that Paul describes the gift of languages as "prayer" (1 Corinthians 14:14) and "thanksgiving" (14:16–17), which builds up the speaker (14:4), and which Paul does himself more than anyone (14:18).

70 Again, this is clearly part of their purpose in the New Testament period (e.g., Hebrews 2:4), but to say that it is the only purpose seems a stretch. Healings are also given for the common good (1 Corinthians 12:7) and for the care of the whole body (12:24–25), as well as—lest we forget—to make sick people better (James 5:14–15). In response to the claim sometimes advanced that miracles in the Old Testament only occurred in specific phases of redemptive history, we need look no further than Jeremiah 32:20 (emphasis added): "You have shown signs and wonders in the land of Egypt, *and to this day in Israel and among all mankind*, and have made a name for yourself, *as at this day*." For the historical development of this particular argument, especially in the work of B. B. Warfield, see Ruthven, *On the Cessation of the Charismata*.

71 It is likely that at least part of the application of Paul's famous body metaphor in 1 Corinthians 12 (cf. also Romans 12:3–8) is that those with prestigious and apparently valuable gifts cannot say to those with other gifts "I have no need of you" (1 Corinthians 12:21). Since all believers risk elevating some gifts above others (Pentecostals might value tongues above administrating, Reformed churches might value teaching above healing, and so on), this is an important challenge for the contemporary church.

said to their friends, "Come, see a man that told me all things that ever I did; beyond a doubt, he must have been sent of God to my soul, or else he could not have described me so exactly." And not only so, but I have known many instances in which the thoughts of men have been revealed from the pulpit. I have sometimes seen persons nudge their neighbours with their elbow, because they had got a smart hit, and they have been heard to say, when they were going out, "The preacher told us just what we said to one another when we went in at the door."[72]

The striking thing about this story is that Spurgeon did not believe that the gift of prophecy was available to him. Yet the phenomenon he describes fits exactly the description that modern charismatics would give of prophecy (and is one I have experienced personally on a number of occasions): he was moved by the Spirit to say something that, though he did not know it at the time, was both timely and accurate, and led to people having the secrets of their hearts exposed and recognizing the presence of God. For me, the best New Testament word to describe this phenomenon would be *prophecy*, or perhaps (as Spurgeon himself implies) *revelation*.[73] But even those who disagree with this can presumably agree on the phenomenon itself, in which the Spirit speaks to us, apart from Scripture, yet without it thereby becoming infallible revelation (not least because our hearing is not as good as it could be).[74] We might even be able to agree that earnestly desiring such things would be helpful, both for the church and for the world she is there to reach.

---

72 Charles Spurgeon, *The Autobiography of Charles H. Spurgeon* (Cincinnati: Curts & Jennings, 1898–1900), 2:226–27.

73 Spurgeon was steeped in Scripture, of course, so it is not surprising that there are echoes of a number of biblical texts in this paragraph, some of which explicitly refer to prophecy (John 4:29; 1 Corinthians 14:25; cp. his remarks on being moved by the Spirit with Acts 13:2; 19:21; 20:22; 21:4).

74 We could say similar things about Augustine's famous conversion story, in which he hears a voice speaking to him, then hears children singing a song that he has never heard, then flicks to a supposedly random page of Scripture, and is saved. Charismatics would be more comfortable using language of "revelation," "prophecy," and "the Spirit speaking" than cessationists or even Augustine himself. But the phenomenon itself is not in question. See Augustine, *Confessions*, Book VIII.

The third argument for pursuing spiritual gifts today, and in my view the most compelling one, is *eschatological*. The gifts of the Spirit, and prophecy in particular, are seen by the apostles as characterizing the entire era between Pentecost and Parousia, the coming of the Spirit and the return of Christ. The kingdom of God is currently spreading throughout the earth like the little stone of Daniel's vision, dethroning kings and crushing empires before it, but it has not yet fully arrived. As long as we still live between the inauguration and the consummation of the kingdom—between D-day and VE-day, in Oscar Cullmann's famous analogy—we should continue to expect, and pursue, all the spiritual gifts.[75]

This expectation is clear on the day of Pentecost itself. These people aren't drunk, explains Peter; they're doing exactly what the prophet Joel predicted: "Your sons and your daughters shall prophesy, and your young men shall see visions, and your old men shall dream dreams; even on my male servants and female servants in those days I will pour out my Spirit, and they shall prophesy."[76] It is interesting that here, right at the start of the first sermon ever preached by a Christian, Peter so explicitly connects the last days, the pouring out of the Spirit on all nations, and the gift of prophecy. The "last days," between the ascension of Jesus and his return, are described in the New Testament as a period of sinfulness in the world and difficulty for the church.[77] But they are also, according to Peter, a period both in which the Spirit is poured out on all flesh and in which male and female, slave and free, will prophesy, see visions, and dream dreams. The latter, in fact, will be a clear sign of the former. So the Pentecost story itself leads us to expect that as long as we are still in "the last days," we should expect the pouring out of the Spirit, accompanied by prophecy.[78]

---

75 Oscar Cullmann, *Christ and Time: The Primitive Christian Conception of Time and History* (London: SCM Press, 1962).

76 Acts 2:17–18.

77 2 Timothy 3:1; James 5:3; 2 Peter 3:3; cf. 1 Corinthians 10:11 (the phrase here is "the end of the ages"); cp. also Hebrews 1:2.

78 For a thorough defense of the idea that the period from Pentecost onward is "the last days" in biblical (and certainly Lukan) theology, see G. K. Beale, *A New Testament Biblical Theology: The*

Paul's letters also affirm that spiritual gifts have been given until the return of Christ. As Paul thanks God for the Corinthians, he reminds them that "the testimony about Christ was confirmed among you—so that *you are not lacking in any gift, as you wait for the revealing of our Lord Jesus Christ*, who will sustain you to the end, guiltless in the day of our Lord Jesus Christ" (1 Corinthians 1:6–8, emphasis added). Paul's gratitude is grounded in past, present, and future realities: the confirmation of the testimony about Christ among them (past), and their possession of spiritual gifts (present) as they wait for the day of the Lord Jesus Christ (future). The *charismata* are theirs while they wait for Jesus to be revealed. Had Paul anticipated the withdrawal of spiritual gifts before the return of Christ, his comments here simply would not have taken this form. It is hard to escape the conclusion that, in Paul's view, spiritual gifts will continue until the end.

Similar things are true of the famous ending to the "love chapter" (which was not originally written as fodder for wedding homilies, but to convince the Corinthians that love was more important, and more permanent, than the spiritual gifts they were so obsessed with): "As for prophecies, they will pass away; as for tongues, they will cease; as for knowledge, it will pass away. For we know in part and we prophesy in part, but when the perfect comes, the partial will pass away."[79] Paul believes in the cessation of the gifts. He believes there is a time when—unlike love, which never ends—they will have served their purpose and will pass away (13:8). As Karl Barth put it, "Because the sun is rising, all lights go out."[80] The question is: When?

The answer is when "the perfect" comes. Paul expresses this in four contrasts: the partial versus the perfect (vv. 9–10), childhood versus maturity (v. 11), dimness of sight versus clarity (v. 12a), and partial knowledge versus fullness (v. 12b). The spiritual gifts are for the age of imperfection, infancy, blurred vision, and partial knowledge; love, on the other hand, will endure even when we experience the perfect,

---

Unfolding of the Old Testament in the New (Grand Rapids: Baker, 2011), 129–60.
79 1 Corinthians 13:8–13.
80 Karl Barth, *The Resurrection of the Dead* (New York: Arno Press, 1977), 81.

adulthood, face-to-face vision, and fullness of knowledge. Prophecy, languages, and knowledge are great for now, but one day we will no longer need them. Why? Because perfection, maturity, and fullness will have come, and we will know face-to-face. Despite occasional exegetical gymnastics to try to prove the contrary, this can only really refer to the return of Christ.[81]

When we read Paul with this eschatological framework in mind—recognizing that believers live in the "last days," between Pentecost and Parousia, characterized both by the gift of the Spirit and the gifts of the Spirit until the return of Christ—we see it everywhere. We notice that the gifts of the ascended Jesus are given to build up his body *"until we all attain to the unity of the faith and of the knowledge of the Son of God, to mature manhood, to the measure of the stature of the fullness of Christ, so that we may no longer be children ..."* (Ephesians 4:13–14, emphasis added). We read that Paul characterizes the present age as one in which believers have been blessed with "every spiritual blessing," which in context presumably includes all the *charismata*.[82] We observe that Paul's exhortation to "be filled with the Spirit," characterized by (among other things) singing "spiritual songs," is given as long as "the days are evil."[83] We notice that the exhortation to use spiritual gifts in Romans applies, like the rest of chapters 12–13, to the period between Jesus's resurrection and return: the time during which believers need not to be conformed to

---

81 The best cessationist interpreters concede this (e.g., Gaffin, *Perspectives on Pentecost*; Schreiner, *Spiritual Gifts*), and the scholarly consensus is extremely strong, as a glance at a random sample of commentaries will indicate; see, e.g., Joseph Fitzmyer, *First Corinthians* (New Haven: Yale, 2008), 498: "It has undoubtedly something to do with the *eschaton* or what Paul calls 'the Day of the Lord' (1:3; 3:13; 5:5) or with the *telos*, 'end' (of the present era), as in 15:24." This case would be further strengthened if, as is very possible, Paul intends in v. 13 to contrast faith and hope, both of which are no longer needed since their goal has been realized, with love, which never ends.

82 Ephesians 1:3. Later in the chapter Paul describes the Spirit as having been given as a deposit until we acquire possession of our full inheritance (13–14) and prays for the Ephesians to be given the Spirit of wisdom, revelation, knowledge, and enlightenment of the mighty power that is at work within them, which raised Christ Jesus from the dead (1:17–21). It is notable that all four of these things (wisdom, revelation, knowledge, and power) are spoken of as *charismata* in 1 Corinthians 12–14; cf. also Colossians 1:9–12.

83 Ephesians 5:15–19.

the pattern of this world, as their salvation gets ever nearer.[84] We see that the command not to quench the Spirit or despise prophecy, likewise, appears in the context of living godly lives as we wait for Jesus to return.[85] Some of these texts are more explicit than others, but it seems clear that Paul anticipates spiritual gifts remaining with the church until the coming of Christ—at which point they will no longer be needed.

Spiritual gifts, in that sense, are like manna. Both manna and spiritual gifts are given for a specific purpose, for a specific period in history. They are meant for people in the wilderness, that awkward period between slavery and promise, Egypt and Canaan, redemption and inheritance. Israel did not need manna in Egypt, because they had melons and garlic. Neither would they need it in the promised land, because they would have milk and honey. (No Israelite, on finally reaching the land after forty years, would think of heading out in the morning to scoop white flakes off the ground; they would be too busy planting crops and harvesting grapes.) In the meantime, however, they needed manna and quail and water from the rock to sustain them on their desert travels.

We too are on a slow and difficult pilgrimage from past rescue to future rest. We have been set free from slavery to sin and death, but we await the day when we can settle in our true homeland. In the past we did not use spiritual gifts, because the Spirit had not yet been poured out. In the new creation we will not need to, because what is mortal will have been swallowed up by life. No Christian, on finally reaching the new creation, will be pursuing gifts of prophecy or languages or healing; we will be too busy worshiping the One to whom all prophecy, language, and healing points. But in the meantime, since the journey is long, God provides us with heavenly presents—which are themselves manifestations of his heavenly presence—to unite us, make us strong, and sustain us on our desert travels.[86]

---

84 Romans 12:3–8, like the rest of Paul's ethical teaching in 12:9–13:10, is sandwiched in between 12:1–2 and 13:11–14, which clearly place it in the context of the church age.

85 1 Thessalonians 5:19–21; cf. 5:1–11, 23–24.

86 These last two paragraphs were originally published in my article, "Our Spiritual Gifts Have an

🔥 🔥 🔥

It should not need to be said (although sadly, it probably does) that the Spirit does not act in conflict with the Word, but only in harmony with the Word, and therefore that we should always pursue spiritual gifts according to the guidelines laid out in the New Testament: that we should weigh prophecies carefully against the testimony of Scripture, bringing correction if needed; that languages should be interpreted or not brought at all; that all gifts should be used to benefit the whole church, not just the individual, and exercised in such a way that enquirers and unbelievers can understand; that giftedness should not circumvent character, recognized church government, or both; that the true test of spirituality should be love for God and love for neighbor, rather than any particular gift or manifestation; that gifts should be used to draw attention to the death and resurrection of Jesus, rather than to any individual, ministry, or church; that prosperity theology should be thoroughly debunked whenever it appears; and that everything should be done in a fitting and orderly way.[87]

Sadly, there are countless examples of these principles being ignored in the contemporary church, with any amount of unbiblical nonsense being justified in the name of being spiritual. Nevertheless, this is an argument for proactive biblical *discernment*, not reactive hesitant *caution*.[88] I find it ironic that perhaps the most common evangelical approach to spiritual gifts, especially in North America, is the one approach that simply cannot be defended from Scripture: that the miraculous gifts continue, but that we should not particularly pursue them! It is possible, and in fact required of us, *both* to earnestly desire spiritual gifts—knowledge, wisdom, faith, prophecy, languages, interpretation, distinguishing spirits, teaching, healing, miracles, helping, administrating, leading, giving, showing

---

Expiration Date," *Christianity Today* (June 2017).

87 In other words, that the numerous parameters given with respect to the exercise of the gifts in 1 Corinthians 12–14 be observed carefully.

88 I owe this distinction to Francis Chan, in personal conversation.

mercy—*and* to do so with scriptural wisdom, so as to build up the body, serve the common good, love one another, and exalt the risen Christ. All these gifts are empowered by one and the same Spirit, who apportions to each one individually as he wills.

There is much more that we could say about all of this, and many have.[89] But for the purposes of this book, the defense rests. The New Testament church was a thoroughly charismatic community, both in their use of spiritual gifts and in their experience of the Holy Spirit himself. Miracles and revelations, angels and demons, dreams and visions were commonplace. When we ask whether the New Testament leads us to expect this to change at the end of the first century or to continue in some form until the return of Christ, it seems there are good historical, hermeneutical, and eschatological reasons for believing the latter. As a result—not in spite of our commitment to the authority of Scripture, but precisely because of it—the church today should continue to zealously desire, and to use, spiritual gifts.

---

89 Books that express the arguments especially well or influentially include the following. On the cessationist side: B. B. Warfield, *Counterfeit Miracles* (Edinburgh: Banner of Truth, 1983); Gaffin, *Perspectives on Pentecost*; Sinclair Ferguson, *The Holy Spirit* (Downers Grove: InterVarsity, 1996); MacArthur, *Strange Fire*; Schreiner, *Spiritual Gifts*. On the continuationist side: D. A. Carson, *Showing the Spirit* (Grand Rapids: Baker, 1987); Ruthven, *On the Cessation of the Charismata*; Jack Deere, *Surprised by the Voice of God* (Grand Rapids: Zondervan, 1996); Fee, *God's Empowering Presence*; Wayne Grudem, *The Gift of Prophecy in the New Testament and Today* (Wheaton: Crossway, 2000). The most useful single volume treatment of the debate remains Wayne Grudem (ed.), *Are Miraculous Gifts for Today?* (Grand Rapids: IVP, 1996), with essays representing cessationist, "Open but Cautious," Third Wave, and Pentecostal perspectives.

CHAPTER 6

EUCHARISMATIC

When You Come Together

Despite the argument of the last five chapters, I am aware that Eucharismatic churches will still sound strange to many. Defensible, perhaps. But strange.

As I write, I am sitting in Dulwich Village in London, looking across the street at a shop that proudly proclaims that it is both a barber shop and a café. From the outside, I cannot imagine why anyone would combine those two things. The speeds, smells, and aesthetics of serving coffee and cutting hair are totally different, and it is hard to think of a more incongruous combination (although I know of a curry house in Streatham that sells Christmas trees, and the comedian Eddie Izzard insists that there is a shop in Tooting Bec that sells guns and banjos, both of which are even more inexplicable). The décor reflects the tension. So does the shop front. What is more, the owners seem to know that their proposition is a baffling fusion: there is a fixed sign outside saying, "Oh Look! A Barbers That Serves Coffee." Yet there it sits. And while I am looking at it, reflecting on the oddity of the hybrid, it suddenly occurs to me: Eucharismatic practice will seem like that to a lot of people. Taken individually, like coffee and haircuts, both elements of it can be defended. But

121

together? Speaking in tongues and set prayers, in the same meeting? Really?

So as we begin this final chapter, on the practicalities of Eucharismatic church life, it is worth reminding ourselves that such a church is not as odd as it sounds. We have been here before, not just historically but biblically. In fact, the New Testament church about whom we know the most, particularly when it comes to their gathered times of worship, was both as eucharistic and as charismatic as they come and provides an excellent starting point for imagining what its Eucharismatic counterparts might look like today. Thank God for the church at Corinth.

Unlike several other New Testament churches, like Jerusalem and probably Rome, the Corinthian congregation was small enough to fit inside one building. We may never know what that building was—a restaurant, a barn, Gaius's house, or something else—but the fact that several of Paul's instructions focus on "when you come together" indicates that the whole church was no more than two hundred strong, and perhaps a lot less.[1] We know that they met in a space that was sufficiently public for visitors, who often were not believers, to join them in worship.[2] In that sense, although there are obviously a large number of differences between the Corinthians and the average contemporary church, there are enough similarities—a common meeting place, socio-economic and ethnic diversity, accessibility to unbelievers, and so on—to make their corporate gatherings instructive for us today.

The Lord's Supper was clearly central. It was a mess, to the extent that Paul thinks it did more harm than good—greed, division, drunkenness, and the rest—but it was central.[3] It seems likely that the

---

1 1 Corinthians 11:17–18, 20, 33–34; 14:23, 26. It is not clear whether Paul's description of Gaius as "host to . . . the whole church" (Romans 16:23) means that he hosted church meetings in his house or hosted traveling missionaries when they came through the city; see the discussion in Edward Adams, *The Earliest Christian Meeting Places: Almost Exclusively Houses?* (London: T&T Clark, 2013).

2 1 Corinthians 14:23–25.

3 To this day, the four main terms used by Protestants to describe the meal come from 1 Corinthians, namely Communion (10:16), breaking of bread (10:16), Lord's Supper (11:20), and Eucharist (11:24).

Eucharist was celebrated each time the church met: Paul begins his correction of their corporate gatherings with a detailed section on it, and of the seven times he says "when you come together," five of them are in the context of sharing Communion. Whether the meeting took place around the table, as suggested by some, or whether it simply included the Supper as a central feature of the liturgy, it is clear that the Corinthian church was eucharistic.

It was also, of course, highly charismatic. The remaining two references to "when you come together" occur in the context of spiritual gifts, with the first distinguishing between the effects of prophecy and languages on unbelievers and the second referring to a wider range of gifts: "What then, brothers? When you come together, each one has a hymn, a lesson, a revelation, a tongue, or an interpretation. Let all things be done for building up" (1 Corinthians 14:26). This provides a fascinating window into Corinthian corporate worship, both in form and in content. In form, because it shows that a large number of people were contributing, and not just the recognized leaders.[4] In content, because it includes singing, teaching, prophesying, language-speaking, and interpreting (and in light of chapter 12, in which distinguishing spirits, miracles, healings, and words of knowledge and wisdom are also mentioned, this list is probably not exhaustive). Then there are the references to not lacking any of the spiritual gifts and to all having been baptized in one Spirit into one body.[5] Despite their many failings, the Corinthians were charismatic with bells on.

It would be possible, in fact, to construct a fairly comprehensive Christian liturgy on the basis of references in 1 Corinthians alone. As well as providing the most extensive biblical material we have on both the Lord's Supper (chapters 10–11) and the *charismata* (12–14), 1 Corinthians also has more to say about preaching (1–2, 9, 15), baptism (1, 10), Christian leadership (3–4), and church discipline (5) than any other letter. We have clear teaching on taking a weekly financial offering (16:1–4), a reference to the church calendar (16:8), and the closest

---

4 I take it that these recognized leaders included Stephanas, Fortunatus, and Achaicus (16:15–18).
5 1 Corinthians 1:7; 12:13.

things the New Testament provides to a creed (8:6; 15:3–8). Abuses of both sacraments—chaos at the Table (11:17–34) and baptism for the dead (15:29–34)—are identified and corrected. More familiarly, we also have greetings from God (1:3) and one another (16:19–21), prayer (1:4–9), ethical teaching (much of chapters 5–10), the preaching of the cross (1:18–2:5) and resurrection (15:1–28), an exhortation based on an Old Testament narrative (10:1–13), liturgical sayings (15:54–55), numerous quotations from Scripture (including the intriguing 4:6), as well as one from the Gospels (7:10–11), an anathema and a maranatha (16:22), and a benediction (16:23). When we compare this with the various liturgical elements we identified in chapter 4, we find that fifteen of the twenty appear in this one letter, and two of the remaining five (namely confession and assurance of forgiveness) appear early in 2 Corinthians.

Admittedly, there are very few of these elements that the Corinthians had not bungled. They were not, in any sense, a model church. Yet the fact that they did these things so badly is ultimately helpful to us: it is the only reason we know about most of them in the first place, and it shows us that Paul felt they were important enough to Christian worship that the Corinthians' practice of each should be corrected rather than abandoned. Some today, on seeing Communion or tongue-speaking or church discipline done badly, solve the problem by dispensing with it altogether. Paul, by contrast, sees the sacraments and gifts of the Spirit precisely as *gifts*, given by a good God for our edification, so his response to such abuses is quite different: "Earnestly desire to prophesy, and do not forbid speaking in tongues. But all things should be done decently and in order" (14:39–40). So if we see the congregation not as it was but as Paul wanted it to be, we have an excellent example of what a Eucharismatic church could look like.

In theory. In practice, things may not be so straightforward.

Granted, if we are planting a new church, then setting a Eucharismatic pattern of worship is not especially complicated. It involves thinking carefully in advance about the use of content (what elements do we want in our liturgy?), space (what physically goes where?), and time (how long do we spend on each element?), but once the shape of corporate worship is broadly agreed upon, it is just a question of implementing it. The church is new, and nobody knows any different, so if you want to use the church calendar, you can. If you want to pursue spiritual gifts together, you can. If you want to start each service with a greeting and a call to worship, then a reading from Scripture, followed by twenty minutes of singing and using the gifts, a creed, five minutes of prayer, another reading from Scripture, confession, assurance, a song, an offering, a twenty minute sermon, silence, the Eucharist, another song, a time of prayer for healing, and then a commission and blessing, you can. It may involve teaching about each element in the early days, so that people understand what is happening and why, but if you start with a blank slate, you can pretty much do what you like.

When a church is already established, however, developing Eucharismatic practice is trickier. We are wrestling with tradition, not just denominationally but congregationally. We are adding practices that some in the church may associate with legalism, lunacy, or both. We are changing our culture as well as our liturgy, which is never easy. The costs of each change are far more obvious: unless we lengthen our meetings indefinitely, which tends to bother everybody (and the children's workers in particular), every five minutes we want to spend doing *this* is five minutes we cannot spend doing *that*. And when people place a high value on doing *that* as much as possible, it is easy to see the reduction of it as a compromise of essential values, rather than a rebalancing act that aims at deepening our worship as a whole. Announce that the Lord's Supper will now be celebrated weekly, and you may hear murmurs of approval. Tell the preacher or the worship leader that they now have ten minutes less than they used to, and the fat will be in the fire.

At the same time, there are a number of practical steps that may make it easier. So, at the risk of turning this chapter into a list of how-tos, here are ten examples. None of them will apply to every

context—the needs of a conservative Bible church moving in a charismatic direction, to take an obvious example, will be very different than
those of a Pentecostal church wanting to embrace the sacraments, and
so on—but all of them will apply to some. In no particular order:

Make the case from Scripture. It sounds obvious, but it still needs
to be said: for any church that takes the Bible as authoritative, there
is no substitute for carefully showing people where, how, and why
Scripture supports a particular practice. Most of us read the Bible as
if it describes individuals and churches just like us, and consequently
we fail to notice the elements of biblical worship that are outside our
experience; when we read about practices that are unfamiliar to us,
we are prone either to relativize them as unique to the New Testament
period or to ignore them completely. (I often think of the young
American woman we met, who heard that people in our church spoke
in tongues. She looked baffled, as if we had recently arrived from
outer space, and then a flicker of recognition passed across her face:
"Tongues? I've read about that. Wait a minute. It's in the Bible!") Many
evangelicals do not register "the public reading of Scripture" as a distinct aspect of Christian worship, since in their experience, Scripture
is only ever read as a preamble to a sermon. Pentecostals may not
notice how liturgical the Psalter is; Presbyterians may not notice how
noisy it is. If our church catechizes people, we will probably pick up
on the fact that Israel did too; if it doesn't, we probably won't.[6] So if
we are hoping to adopt a new practice, one of our primary tasks will
be to show that it is biblical. This will not always be sufficient—old
habits die hard—but it will always be necessary.

Make the case from history. If faced with the choice between
reformation and revolution, choose reformation.[7] The sales pitch is
harder—there is an undeniable appeal to overthrowing the old and
pioneering something completely new, whereas the call to make

---

6 E.g., Exodus 13:14–15; Deuteronomy 6:20–25; Joshua 4:6–7.

7 The pragmatic reason for this is the plot of George Orwell's *Animal Farm* or, for that matter, the
French Revolution: every successful revolt ends with a new establishment, so the overthrow-
er eventually becomes the overthrowee. The theological reason is the unity of the church, on
which see chapter 4.

things a bit better by returning to our roots sounds a bit tame, even insipid, in comparison—but by stressing the unity of the people of God across the generations, an emphasis on continuity both honors the church of the past and strengthens the church of the future.

The classic example is John Calvin. Writing in a context when it would have been easy to trumpet the Reformation's radical newness and throw the previous fifteen centuries under the bus, Calvin did the opposite, arguing that the Reformers were actually far closer to the church fathers than his Roman Catholic contemporaries were:

> Our agreement with antiquity is far closer than yours, [and] all we have attempted has been to renew that ancient form of the Church. . . . Place, I pray, before your eyes, that ancient form of the Church, such as their writings prove it to have been in the age of Chrysostom and Basil, among the Greeks, and of Cyprian, Ambrose, and Augustine, among the Latins; after so doing, contemplate the ruins of that Church, as now surviving among yourselves."[8]

He put it elsewhere in even stronger terms: "Augustine is completely ours."[9] In the same way, though it is tempting to regard being Eucharismatic as a courageous act of novelty, it is wiser and more accurate to regard it as a simple act of fidelity, as I have attempted to show in this book.

Take your time. Most people struggle with cultural change, so we need not only great wisdom but also great patience when leading any community or organization through it.[10] It takes time. And the more integral something is to a community's identity—and few things define our corporate identity more than our worship practices—the

---

8 John Calvin, *Reply to Sadoleto.*

9 John Calvin, *Concerning the Eternal Predestination of God.* In light of Augustine's theology of gift, the sacraments, and miracles, I think it can be pressed into service in a Eucharismatic context as well.

10 Paperbacks on change management proliferate, so there is no need to expand on that theme here (although I suspect that more often than not, people who read books on change management are in a different part of the Venn Diagram to people who read books like this).

longer it takes to change. I often think of Martin Luther, eager to press forward with the Reformation in Wittenberg, but waiting until 1523 before altering the Latin Mass and not producing a German Mass until 1526, a remarkable nine years after publishing the ninety-five theses. Luther wanted liturgical change, but he also knew how unsettling people would find it, so he gave them time.[11] There is pastoral wisdom there.

Cast a compelling vision. Leading through any kind of change requires vision-casting. If people are not caught up with a picture of a better future, and motivated to act in order to make it a reality, they will almost always stay as they are.[12] Those leading churches in a charismatic direction will often see this instinctively, because vision-casting is often part of the culture and language of such churches, and there are plenty of good examples to follow.[13] But it is important when leading in a eucharistic direction as well. I remember the power of hearing Peter Leithart paint a picture of what he calls Reformational Catholicism, and desperately wanting in on it, despite not being entirely sure what to do next.[14] I have been deeply shaped by the eucharistic visions of church life cast by people like Eugene

---

11 I owe this point to Professor Carl Trueman.

12 The exceptions that prove the rule are those occasions when so much power is concentrated in one person, or group of people, that change can simply be imposed from above, and everyone has to lump it. This is hopefully rare in modern church life—although interestingly it is exactly how we ended up with the Book of Common Prayer, arguably the finest liturgy to have been written in any language.

13 One thinks of leaders like John Wimber, Terry Virgo, Sandy Miller, Sam Storms, Francis Chan, Tope Koleoso, Matt Chandler, and many others.

14 "Being a Reformational Catholic Christian is a circus ride, a high-wire act with no net but the loving arms of our faithful Father. If you suffer from vertigo, or are pregnant, it might not be the place for you; you may want to find a safer ride. . . . I long to see churches that neglect the Eucharist blasted from the earth. I hope to see fragmented Protestantism, anti-liturgical, anti-sacramental Protestantism, thinly biblical Protestantism, anti-doctrinal, anti-intellectual Protestantism, anti-traditional Protestantism, rationalist and nationalist Protestantism, slip into the grave—and I'll be there to help to turn that grave into a dancefloor . . . But death is never the last word for the church of the living God, the God who is faithful to death, and then again, faithful. Christianity and future are synonymous, and if Protestant churches must die, they die in faith that they will be raised new, more radiant with glory than ever. For the Creator who said in the fifth and the ninth and the sixteenth century, 'It is good,' will not finish his work until we come to the final Sabbath, where everything will, once and for all, be very, very good." "The Future of Protestantism: A Conversation with Peter Leithart, Fred Sanders, and Carl Trueman," Biola University, 29 April 2014.

Peterson, James K. A. Smith, Michael Horton, N. T. Wright, and Tim Keller (though they all differ, and I imagine none of them would put it like that).[15] Most formative of all, for me, has been the mischievous, chortling influence of G. K. Chesterton, with his stridency, paradoxes, and almost Eucharismatic penchant for both traditions and miracles, repetition and supernaturalism, dogmas and fairy tales.[16] In each case the impulse toward sacramental, liturgical, or historical worship has come more through an appeal to the imagination than a logical argument. Once again: we are what we love.

Pick low-hanging fruit first. Some historic practices are easier to swallow than others. Some spiritual gifts are easier to use corporately than others. In the vast majority of cases, people will not respond well to being introduced to the most unfamiliar, fully caffeinated practice first; announcing out of the blue that there is now an open prophecy microphone, or a weekly recited prayer in Tudor English, is likely to do more harm than good.[17] In most churches, however, there will be a more accessible equivalent, and this is the place to start. In a Pentecostal context it might be a biblical blessing ("May the Lord bless you and keep you . . .") or doxology ("Now to him who is able to do immeasurably more than all we ask or imagine . . .") or very short creed ("Christ has died! Christ has risen! Christ will come

---

15 E.g., Eugene Peterson, *The Contemplative Pastor* (Grand Rapids: Eerdmans, 1993); Smith, *You Are What You Love*; Michael Horton, *Ordinary: Sustainable Faith in a Radical, Restless World* (Grand Rapids: Zondervan, 2014); N. T. Wright, *Surprised by Hope* (London: SPCK, 2007), 267–302; Tim Keller, *Center Church* (Grand Rapids: Zondervan, 2012), 249–383.

16 For instance, I doubt if anyone has cast a more compelling vision for the repetitive nature of liturgical worship—without even intending to!—than this: "Because children have abounding vitality, because they are in spirit fierce and free, therefore they want things repeated and unchanged. They always say, 'Do it again'; and the grown-up person does it again until he is nearly dead. For grown-up people are not strong enough to exult in monotony. But perhaps God is strong enough to exult in monotony. It is possible that God says every morning, 'Do it again' to the sun; and every evening, 'Do it again' to the moon. It may not be automatic necessity that makes all daisies alike; it may be that God makes every daisy separately, but has never got tired of making them. It may be that He has the eternal appetite of infancy; for we have sinned and grown old, and our Father is younger than we" (Chesterton, *Orthodoxy*, 216–17).

17 A classic example of the latter is Thomas Cranmer's use of "miserable sinners," which has probably done more than any other phrase to convince people that Anglicanism is irretrievably gloomy. Given that the Latin *miserere nobis* means "have mercy upon us," it is likely that "miserable" in 1552 meant "in need of mercy" rather than "sad"—but that point is probably lost on the majority of people who say it today.

again!"). In a liturgically skeptical yet conservative church it might be the Lord's Prayer or the Grace or a declaration following the reading of Scripture ("This is the word of God"). Communion opens up all sorts of possibilities, before ("On the night he was betrayed . . ."), during ("the body of Christ . . .") and after ("thank you for feeding us . . ."). Preaching through a creed or confession may, counterintuitively, be less alien to people than reciting one. Even the creeds and confessions themselves vary in the extent to which people today can access them. The Apostles' Creed is shorter, and more amenable to congregational use, than the Nicene Creed, let alone the Athanasian Creed. The Heidelberg Catechism is warmer, more personal, and more ecumenical than the Westminster Catechisms.[18] By thinking carefully about the accessibility of any new liturgical elements we are introducing, we can demystify a step that many would otherwise find strange.

The same is true of spiritual gifts. Most Western Christians, if asked to sketch a spectrum from the most accessible and familiar spiritual gifts at one end to the most unsettling and edgy at the other, would give roughly the same results, whether we are charismatic or not. Everyone is happy with helping, administrating, encouraging, and teaching. Most of us are fine with leadership, showing mercy, and giving. Whether we feel comfortable with words of wisdom and knowledge, distinguishing spirits, and the gift of faith, will depend largely on what we think they are. Healing is something that most Christians are happy to pray for, even if they are not convinced the gift of healing still exists. If we move into prophecy or miracles, we will find a lot more controversy about whether, and how, they should be practiced. And if we start speaking in or interpreting languages, we will find some people saying of us, as friends of mine say of me, that we are simply delusional.

The existence of such a spectrum is interesting in itself, given that it does not appear in Scripture at all.[19] Yet it can help us when it

---

18 Though often championed by Calvinists, the Heidelberg Catechism also has the distinction of being the work most often given away to people by Jacob Arminius.

19 Different people will regard the spectrum as evidence of the rightness of their position. Cessationists will argue that the controversial ones are all linked to the ministry of the apostles

comes to cultural change. Making time to pray for the sick at the end of a service, laying on hands, and anointing them with oil, is a much easier place to start than making time for prophetic ministry in the middle of it. And prophecy is, in turn, more accessible to people than languages and interpretation; most people will be far happier with a pastor having a spontaneous insight into the situation of someone in the congregation—like Charles Spurgeon did, as we saw earlier— than with someone shouting out in tongues in between songs. To recognize this is not to foist such a continuum onto Paul (for whom, as we know, prophecy was the gift to be pursued "especially"), but rather to acknowledge a practical reality in the contemporary West.[20] We can then respond accordingly.

Distinguish between "deep end" and "shallow end" contexts.[21] It can be helpful to use the image of a swimming pool to differentiate between the various sorts of meetings that a church might hold and the implications that has for the use of spiritual gifts. A Sunday morning service would be "shallow end": there are lots of visitors, new people, and unbelievers present—many of whom have not yet learned to swim, charismatically speaking—so you need to be careful not to drown them. In practice, that means making the meeting as safe as possible, explaining things carefully, and preventing it from descending into a charismatic free-for-all. A midweek prayer meeting, by contrast, might be "deep end": there are few if any visitors, no unbelievers, and virtually everyone there is a committed member of the church. As such, you can afford to be more open and take more risks, since you know everyone

---

in ways that the others are not, which only proves that charismatics don't know their Bibles; charismatics will respond that the uncontroversial ones are all things that unbelievers can do, which only shows that cessationists want to do without the Spirit altogether. There is a self-reinforcing feedback loop at work, too, as the excesses of some prompt greater levels of caution in others (see, you guys are all crazy!), which accentuates the excesses (see, you guys have no power!), and so on. See also the excellent reflection from John Piper, "Why Some Spiritual Gifts Attract Unstable People," in *A Godward Life: Seeing the Supremacy of God in All of Life* (Sisters: Multnomah, 1997), 131–33.

20 As those who have traveled in the Majority World will know, the spectrum does not look the same (or even exist!) in every culture.

21 I owe this language to Dr. Dave Smith, pastor of KingsGate Community Church in Peterborough.

can swim. The upshot of this is that "deep end" contexts are very help-ful for growing in the use of spiritual gifts, since they allow for people to try, fail, learn from their mistakes, and try again.

I suspect the same is true of liturgical innovation, although the "deep end" contexts might be different. Some are made possible by the church calendar. Advent, Christmas, Lent, Good Friday, Easter Sunday, and Pentecost all lend themselves to a focus on, or develop-ment of, specific worship practices. Since "we do not know what to pray for as we ought," prayer meetings can be good contexts in which to introduce set prayers to help us, whether from the Psalms, Jesus, the apostles, or the history of the church. There is also an opportu-nity to use liturgy in formal settings, like weddings and funerals, that does not exist in more everyday contexts, an opportunity that is enhanced by the fact that traditional wedding and funeral liturgies are so beautifully crafted and so well known in the culture at large ("to have and to hold," "ashes to ashes," and so on).

Don't underestimate the power of music. A couple of years ago, I was asked by a church leader if I had any advice on how to get anti-liturgical charismatics to engage with the creeds. "Use music," I replied. "If you have someone playing a pad sound on the keyboard in the background, charismatics will do anything." I was joking, obviously—but only just. I have seen nonliturgical congrega-tions reciting the Nicene Creed in worship, raising their hands, and applauding at the end, because the presence of background music made it *feel* like a worship environment rather than an empty ritual. Countless others have started making public declarations about their belief in the Trinity, the virgin birth, and the communion of saints thanks to Hillsong.[22] The use of music has made all sorts of churches more eucharistic, quite literally, by accompanying the bread and wine and thereby communicating to the congregation that this is an act of worship, not formalism.

By the same token, music has helped many to become more char-ismatic. Partly this is practical. It is tricky, to say nothing of incredibly

---

22 "This I Believe (The Creed)," by Ben Fielding and Matt Crocker.

awkward, to dance without music—if you don't believe me, try it—and difficult in many cultures to shout without music, so if we are committed to expressing the full heights of joy we looked at in chapter 3, we will find music is indispensable. It is also theological. As anyone who has read the Old Testament will know, music has always played a central role not just in expressing joy and encouraging thanksgiving, but also in entering God's presence, conquering the enemy, and in one fascinating story, making prophecy possible.[23] Paul sings with his spirit as well as his mind and urges believers to sing "spiritual songs" with thankfulness to God.[24] When he tells the Ephesians to be filled with the Spirit, he lists four examples of what that will look like, and two of them involve music.[25] So if a church is asking how to move in a more charismatic direction, music will almost certainly be part of the answer.

Cultivate Eucharismatic lives as pastors and lay leaders. If you want to change the culture of an organization, you will almost always need to change the culture of the leadership. God has structured reality such that pastors and lay leaders reproduce their lives, habits, and emphases throughout the churches they lead. If you are not in leadership, that can be enormously frustrating. If you are, however, it is enormously encouraging, because it indicates that the most helpful thing to do, if you are hoping to pastor people through cultural change, is to embody the change yourself. If your pastoral or staff teams and volunteer teams use spiritual gifts when they pray together—words of wisdom or encouragement, prophecy, languages, interpretations, prayer for healing, or whatever—then it will spread, whether you mean for it to or not. If, like me, you draw on Cranmer to help you pray, you get excited about the Lord's Supper whenever you share it, and your wife has Post-it notes with portions of the Heidelberg Catechism on the kitchen wall, you will likely find that the people you pastor are shaped by it, even if you never tell them

23 1 Chronicles 15:16–28; 2 Chronicles 20:20–23; 2 Kings 3:14–20.
24 1 Corinthians 14:15; Colossians 3:16.
25 Ephesians 5:18–21.

about it. Leadership is like that. The Greek proverb says it best: "The fish stinks from the head down."[26]

Use spiritual gifts within biblical parameters. If you want to put people off spiritual gifts for life, practice them unbiblically. Put contemporary prophecy on a par with Scripture. Teach that tongues are the primary measurement of spirituality, and that they should be used in public meetings whether or not they are interpreted, preferably all at once. Emphasize the signs more than the person they are pointing to, your spiritual experiences more than the love of your neighbor, and spiritual fireworks more than whether enquirers can understand what's going on. Connect spiritual blessings to financial gifts wherever possible. Promise people that they will always be healed or see the miracle they need, if they have enough faith. Ensure that no tongue-speaker ever interprets their own language. Test nothing. Make it clear that healings and miracles validate a person's interpretation of Scripture, so if you want to know whether someone is theologically correct, just look at whether they have the gift of healing. Build the church or ministry around a personality, with minimal accountability. If anyone challenges you on any of this, wave them away as carnal or legalistic or both.

Alternatively, we can practice them biblically, with careful attention paid to the teaching of the apostles in general and 1 Corinthians 12–14 in particular. Boundaries are for our benefit. Guardrails are gifts.

Tell your story as catholically as possible. Our natural tendency when putting ourselves on the map, whether as individuals, families, tribes, or nations, is to emphasize all the things that make us distinctive. Local churches are no different. We are so inclined to see ourselves as the end to which the rest of church history has been building that we tell our story that way, highlighting the things we do that others don't, the things we have found that others have missed. If we are not careful, the whole thing can become a marketing exercise: our values can become a brand identity, our vision statement a USP (unique selling proposition), and whoever gains the most market share wins.

---

26 This could easily be an epithet for 1–2 Kings.

Yet we believe in one holy, catholic, and apostolic church. We who are many are one body, because we all share in one bread. We are not competitors, like McDonald's and Burger King; we are partners, relatives, family members. There are some obvious differences between us, and they matter, but the things we have in common matter far more. So we need to tell our story with catholicity and clarity and charity and joy. To that end, the most helpful tool I have encountered is the distinction between the things that are written in pencil, in ink, and in blood.[27]

I have all kinds of theological beliefs and all kinds of regular practices. Some of them are written in pencil: I can articulate them and explain them, but they are somewhat provisional, and if at some point I had to rub them out and replace them with something else, it wouldn't make that much difference. Some of them—my position on baptism or spiritual gifts or church government—are written in ink. These are things I believe or practice that I would put my name to and defend with some conviction; admittedly, I could still be wrong about them, since many of my brothers and sisters disagree with me, but I really don't think I am, and I would probably not be able to thrive in a church that didn't share them. Some of my convictions, however, are written in blood. These things—the Nicene Creed, the Ten Commandments, the Lord's Prayer—are the things I would die for, and many have. They are the truly important things that, if you take them away, turns Christianity into something else. On these, I am one with the entire church throughout history. We believe in one God. We believe in the Trinity. We believe Jesus died for our sins and rose again from the dead. We will not worship any other gods. Here we stand, we can do no other.

So our story is not a tale of how we came to be right when everyone else was wrong (although we obviously think we *are* right; everybody does). It is rather a story of one church, with one mission, united by blood, of which our local congregation is a small but vital

---

27 Keith Drury, "My Own Faith Meltdown Story" (http://www.drurywriting.com/keith/faith.melt-down.story.htm).

part. We have reasons for doing things a certain way, just as others have reasons for doing things another way. We love God and love our neighbors like this because we honestly believe it is the best way of enjoying the grace of God, and here's how we got here, and here's why we think that, and we don't apologize for it. We do, though, acknowledge that one day all our inky distinctives will disappear, and there will be one flock and one shepherd. In the meantime: welcome.

In the course of writing this, I have been asked by a number of people which church(es) best embody the vision I am trying to cast, and I never know what to tell them. As far as I know, there is no Platonic, perfect form of a Eucharismatic church out there, taking these elements of history, experience, liturgy, miracle, and sacrament, and binding them all together in perfect harmony. Sometimes ecclesial adjectives are binary: a local church either is, or is not, "Presbyterian," "multisite," "nonconformist," or whatever. But usually they form a spectrum: "sacramental," "charismatic," "diverse," "evangelical," "missional," and so on. Adjectives like this are end points, not starting points. They tell you what a congregation is reaching for, as opposed to what it already is.

"Eucharismatic" is like that. It is aspirational, not descriptive. It indicates a desire to make the most of all the gifts God has given to the church, but it doesn't specify a particular way of doing it. In some contexts it may mean deciding to celebrate the Eucharist on a Sunday occasionally or monthly or weekly. In others it might involve making space to pray for healing at the end of a service. In others, it could look like incorporating a prayer of confession, a prophecy, a creed, or a language into corporate worship for the first time. It could make some churches louder, some churches quieter, and some churches both.

Yet for all that the practice will look different, depending on the context, the motive will always be the same. To be Eucharismatic is to have our minds persuaded, and our hearts captivated, by this biblical and historical reality: the Triune God has showered his church with gifts, and every one of them is good, and we will maximize our joy (*chara*) and our appreciation of his grace (*charis*) as we receive and treasure all of them. It may sound like a tall order. But if Paul could envisage the Corinthians, with all their problems, holding fast to the traditions they received, sharing in the Lord's body and blood when they came together and lacking no spiritual gifts as they waited for Jesus to return, then it should be possible for anyone.[28]

Receiving some of these gifts will be more comfortable than others. Some of them will be a familiar part of our tradition, and some of them won't. But if they are given by the Father of lights, from whom every good and perfect gift comes and with whom there is no shadow or variation due to change, then although we need wisdom, we need not fear.[29] God is good, all the time. All the time, God is good. "If you then, who are evil, know how to give good gifts to your children, how much more will your Father who is in heaven give good things to those who ask him!" (Matthew 7:11).

Grace be with you.

---

28 1 Corinthians 1:7–8; 11:2; 10:14–22; 11:17–34.
29 James 1:17.

ACKNOWLEDGMENTS

I am grateful to all kinds of people for the privilege of being able to write books, but first on the list are the wonderful people of King's Church London, who not only give me the time to read and write, but also allow me to preach into, talk about, and actually practice many of the things described in these pages. Since I joined the team in 2016, Steve and Deb Tibbert have gone above and beyond what we could have hoped for; Phil Varley and Tris Newman have been great supports, great colleagues, and great friends; and more people than I can count have encouraged me as a pastor and welcomed me as a person (Lavern, Brett, Cindy, Sarah, Jonathan, Shani, Farriea, Mike and Sus, William and Hilary, Simon and Becs, and around fifteen hundred others). Thank you, everyone.

A number of friends have contributed to this specific project with their insights, wisdom, writings, feedback, or sheer example: Matt Anderson, Josh Butler, Matt Chandler, Donnie Griggs, Matt Hosier, Tope Koleoso, Guy Miller (whose prophetic word for me got the ball rolling), Trillia Newbell, Glenn Packiam, Jennie Pollock, Derek Rishmawy, P-J Smyth, Sam Storms, Jon Tyson, Joel Virgo, Evan Wickham, Jen Wilkin, and a host of others whose presence in the footnotes will attest to their influence. When you are going out on a limb on something (or, at least, when it feels like you are), it is wonderful to look around and see all sorts of other Eucharismatics pursuing the same things, whether they use that word or not. Where things in this book were insightful, thank them; where things in this book were indefensible, blame me. The same could also be said of the remarkably thorough and empathic editing of Madison Trammel and Bob Hudson, and of the whole team at Zondervan, who have been thoughtful, understanding, and professional throughout.

As ever, though, it is Rachel who makes the most sacrifices when I write anything—especially when I am trying to hit a fairly optimistic deadline!—and spends the most time reading it, talking about it, and encouraging me in it, so she is the one who deserves the most thanks. Every good and perfect gift comes from above . . .